Chalkboards
and Clipboards

Chalkboards and Clipboards

My Thirty-Five Years at The Montgomery Academy

Tommy Jones

iUniverse, Inc.
Bloomington

Chalkboards and Clipboards
My Thirty-Five Years at The Montgomery Academy

iUniverse books may be ordered through booksellers or by contacting:

iUniverse
1663 Liberty Drive
Bloomington, IN 47403
www.iuniverse.com
1-800-Authors (1-800-288-4677)

Because of the dynamic nature of the Internet, any web addresses or links contained in this book may have changed since publication and may no longer be valid. The views expressed in this work are solely those of the author and do not necessarily reflect the views of the publisher, and the publisher hereby disclaims any responsibility for them.

Any people depicted in stock imagery provided by Thinkstock are models, and such images are being used for illustrative purposes only.
Certain stock imagery © Thinkstock.

ISBN: 978-1-4620-1345-6 (sc)
ISBN: 978-1-4620-1347-0 (hc)
ISBN: 978-1-4620-1346-3 (ebk)

Printed in the United States of America

iUniverse rev. date: 09/14/2011

Contents

To Steve and Julibeth;

to the seventy-eight Middle School girls whom I was
honored to have coached;

and to the students who I enjoyed teaching so much.

ACKNOWLEDGMENTS

Gene Johnson, who got me started on this journey down memory lane.

Wade Segrest, who checked for historical accuracy.

Mirenda Tatum, who had the unenviable task of correcting all my grammatical errors.

Attorney Dennis Bailey, who reviewed this book for any litigation issues.

Doc Holladay, without whose technological help this book would never have been published.

1

ADMINISTRATORS

This is not meant to be a historical document, but rather my perspective and memories created in my thirty-five years at The Montgomery Academy (MA)—some personally experienced and others recounted to me by others. In some cases, names have been omitted to prevent further embarrassment.

After fifteen years of teaching in public schools, I was hired by Wade Segrest, Headmaster at the time. He told me later that he selected me over two other candidates who had doctoral degrees. I know I had strong support from two board members, Charlie Stakely and Dr. Buddy Freeman. At the same time, my son, Steve, was accepted into the seventh grade (it was called "form" in those days). He likes to say that they took me to get him, while I tell him that it was the opposite. Regardless, it was an awesome treat to drive back and forth each day with him. Thus, in the fall of 1976 began thirty-five wonderful, cherished years at a place I grew to dearly love.

A major attraction at MA at the time was the lack of clerical work required of teachers. Teachers were expected to prepare and to teach, not to do paperwork or "computer work." We were on the quarter system, with exams prior to Thanksgiving and spring holidays and at the end of the year. Report cards were issued at the end of each quarter, and we made reports every six weeks. The only other time teachers reported to parents was when a student failed a test. Then the dreaded "yellow slip" was sent home.

Over those years, there were seemingly endless changes. Let me mention a few that have taken place.

The staff consisted of Headmaster Wade; assistant Headmaster Ken Dyess; one full-time secretary known as the legend, Joyce Sweatt; one half-time secretary; Susan Shirock, the director of the Lower School; one guidance/college admissions counselor; one custodian; and one maintenance man, Gerald Bowles. They got it all done, despite the fact that grades K–12 were all located on the one campus in Montgomery, Alabama. Of course, the physical plant was nothing to compare with what we have today.

The curriculum was much more nuts-and-bolts. The last time I counted there were ninety-plus offerings in the Upper School, some with as few as two or three pupils.

Admissions standards were much more stringent, and there was a much more select group of students.

Teacher appearance in terms of dress for ladies and men was not as liberal. For example, male teachers wore ties every day.

Technology consisted of dial telephones, typewriters, and one or two 16mm movie projectors, which teachers had to sign up for.

As with admission standards, academic standards were different.

There was a true Honor Code System. Teachers would hand out tests or exams and leave the room.

Discipline was tighter. There were pranks and misbehavior, but punishment was swift, consistent, and appropriate for the misdeed.

Each teacher was expected to provide an appropriate devotional and lead in the Pledge of Allegiance each day.

The dining service was "home-owned." We had fried chicken each Wednesday and yeast rolls every day. On most days, three or four mailmen would come in to eat, paying one dollar. Of course, we did not have nearly the food choices afforded the students today.

One amusing anecdote from my first year at MA dealt with the custodian. I never knew his last name. He went by "Thomas," and he was ancient. Let's just say that he was not a poster child for high energy. There was a dead roach in the corner by the door to the administrative office. It stayed there one full week.

I spent all thirty-five years teaching seventh-grade life science and about half of those years also teaching biology until the school became too large for one teacher to do both. Given the choice of subjects, I chose the seventh graders, although at the time my heart was with the tenth graders. I was advised to do so by one who knew that "I would not like the direction that the Upper School was going." Second only to my decision to come to MA, selecting the seventh grade was a wonderful decision for myself as I grew to love the seventh graders even more than I already did, and I found teaching them to be so rewarding. Certainly, there were problems, but they were quite different from the problems I could have faced with older students.

Coach classes were a new innovation for me. Teachers set up help times for students desiring further instruction. Any students failing a test were required to attend coach class. Coach class took precedence over any extracurricular activities, including athletics. This is still true today.

Although most coach classes were and are held after school, my personal philosophy was that by 3:15, or 3:05 as it was, a student's brains were pretty much fried and had had enough school for one day, so I had my coach classes in the mornings before school while minds were still fresh.

Teachers did not, and still do not, have tenure. We had to prove ourselves each year, which is the way all schools, including public schools, should operate. Also, there was no salary schedule. You were paid according to what the school could afford and what the Headmaster judged you were worth. One-year contracts were the standard.

At some point soon, Joe Kirk became the custodian. Every night, Joe would clean each classroom, empty all wastebaskets, and wash every blackboard, K–12. Also, if anyone wanted to know what was going on at MA, they could ask Joe. He even knew about the "demon-possessed" senior trailer.

Wade was the perfect administrator for the type of school MA was originally conceived to be—a school meant exclusively for only the very top students. He was a very good businessman. School finances were on good footing. Wade took care of his faculty, never showing any favoritism toward any of us. He was a strong supporter of all the extracurricular activities at the school, not just the ones his children were involved in. If there was an event at the school, Wade was there, often with his wife. When the trustees decided to add a section, Wade warned that, in doing so, MA would have to have less-qualified students in order to fill the classes, and that this would result in lowered standards in order to keep the lower achievers in school. He was right on both counts.

I remember so well two of Wade's quotes. Referring to a child with problems, academic or behavioral, he would say, "The acorn does not fall too far from the tree." The other one came at a preschool faculty meeting in which Wade told us, "Try to make some child happy, and smile every day." Since then, I always tried to do that.

As an aside, some of the students privately called Wade "Fuddy." Because he would not permit something they wanted to do, they said he was an old fuddy duddy.

Following Wade's resignation, Dr. Al Kerr was brought on board as interim Headmaster. Dr. Kerr had a very good reputation, and part of his responsibility was to prune the faculty of what was perceived to be dead wood. He turned out to be a huge disappointment. Not only did he fail to accomplish what he was supposed to do, but about all he did all day was sit in his office, smoke, and write letters.

Robin Byrd became MA's new Headmaster. His "coronation" was held at a convocation at the Davis Theater where he was presented with a pair of track shoes so he could hit the ground running. Mr. Byrd was a young man in his first tenure as a Headmaster. His daughter, Anne Lane, was a sweet young lady and a fine student. As in the case of Wade Segrest, Robin Byrd did not attempt to curry special favors for his child. Also, as with Wade, Mr. Byrd's wife was a strong supporter of the school, but she stayed in the background.

When Mr. Byrd assumed his position, the school was undergoing a massive renovation to remove asbestos. Teachers had to pack up everything in their classrooms for storage, and all rooms, including the administrative suite, were completely emptied out.

Mr. Byrd smoked like a chimney. He once remarked that it would probably save him five years at "The Home." Mr. Byrd had a tie with "MCP" (Male Chauvinist Pig) on it. The story is that he said that his worst male teacher was better than his best female teacher. *Ouch!*

'Twas said that Mr. Byrd did not like old people. I cannot comment on that because, at the time, I was not old, and I got along fine with him. We had a cordial, professional relationship, and he was always accessible whenever I needed him.

Mr. Byrd's tenure marked the first major attempt to bring diversification to the student body. By and large, this was not successful because too many of the students were not qualified academically and did not blend well socially. I felt it was unfair to these youngsters to take them from their comfort zone during the day and then return them to their neighborhoods after school each day. It was not a formula for happiness and success.

Mr. Byrd's legacy was the beautiful new Lower School campus. But with it came the expanded enrollment. Mr. Byrd was quoted as saying, "We have to put bodies in those desks."

He displayed a unique way of letting a teacher know he or she was not going to be rehired. On one occasion, a group of eight teachers was seated at a table in the lunchroom eating lunch. Mr. Byrd came in and passed out contracts to seven of them.

My favorite quote from Mr. Byrd was, "Every student has the right to fail, and you as teachers do not have the right to take that away from them if that is what they choose to do." Unfortunately, I allowed myself to get away from that for a while. I lowered classroom standards so less-qualified students could pass.

Following Mr. Byrd's departure, Assistant Headmaster Paul Feakins became interim Headmaster. I am afraid the best thing I can say about Mr. Feakins is that he had a very nice family. In my opinion, he was arrogant with absolutely nothing to be arrogant about. After one of our seniors was accepted to SMU, he made the statement, "I got _____ into S.M.U." I guess her record and sterling character had nothing to do with it.

At his first faculty meeting, he made the statement that every teacher would get an $800 raise the following year, and anything above that would let the teacher know what he thought about him or her. He told John Tatum, "Now I have you where I want you." John replied, "Hoss, I'll be here when you are gone."

He applied for the position of Headmaster, asking the two members of the search committee to write letters of recommendation for him. I presume they both supported him anyway, but this seemed a highly unethical request. After all, what choice did they really have?

I will praise Mr. Feakins for one specific occurrence. One night, a car full of guys decided to egg his house. He ran outside, hurling eggs at their rapidly retreating car.

Dr. Emerson Johnson became our new Headmaster. At six feet seven inches tall, he was an individual you looked up to in more ways than one. Dr. Johnson was the polar opposite of Mr. Feakins in personality and people skills. He came in as the consummate professional, and his wife continued the tradition of staying in the background and supporting her husband and the faculty.

A specific example of how kind Dr. Johnson could be occurred when I rear-ended another car, causing my car to go on the disabled list for a few days. Dr. Johnson loaned me his car during that time.

He began the faculty retreats prior to the opening of school. The retreats were funded by the POA (Parents of the Academy). We faculty would spend two or three days off campus preparing for the beginning of the new school year.

As with any new person in charge, there were the inevitable changes. Dr. Johnson actively promoted diversity. Some of these results were positive, others not so.

For years a rival school, St. James, had monopolized children of officers at the military bases, thanks to their Headmaster, a retired general, Raymond Furlong. Dr. Johnson actively and successfully began recruiting these students.

By this time, 1998, we had gone to the semester system with final exams prior to the Christmas holidays. Over the objections of just about everyone, Dr. Johnson set up the midterm exams for after the Christmas holidays. To give Dr. Johnson credit, if something proved unsuccessful, he was willing to change as he did in this case, reversing his decision after a year or so. No one had wanted exams hanging over their heads during the Christmas holidays.

Another major change was unannounced and sprung on everyone. If the Middle School director had not pointed this out at a faculty meeting, it might have been some time before anyone found out that Dr. Johnson had banished exemptions from final exams. Previously, students with an "A" average were not required to take the final exam, although all did have to take the midterm exams. This did cause a furor. In a meeting, the Middle School faculty voted overwhelmingly, with only three dissenting votes, to restore exemptions. This did not happen until the following year, and even then the exemptions were diluted, with ninth and tenth graders not being eligible for exemptions. One typical example occurred with one of my more capable seventh graders. During the second semester, she was making Bs instead of her customary As. When I asked her about it, her reply was, "What for? I cannot be exempt."

Passing at MA had always been an average of 70 or above. Dr. Johnson did not like having to defend an F with a grade of 69 to parents, so the unwritten policy became to find good cause to lower the grade to 68 or bump it to 70. In other words, passing now became a 69 or above. I loved Diane Blondheim's philosophy when she became Middle School director: "Sixty-nine is not seventy so it is an F." We never had grades of D at MA, until later when Mr. Douglas became Headmaster.

Dr. Johnson insisted on sportsmanship from the coaches and players. If a player got a technical foul, he or she had a conference with Dr. Johnson and had to sit out the first half of the next game. If a coach drew a technical foul or if his or her conduct on the sidelines was not acceptable, then the coach was called in. If the conduct continued, the coach would be dismissed. He also expected coaches to dress appropriately for games. In other words, he exhibited strong leadership and expected MA coaches to be examples of good sportsmanship and role models for their charges.

On one occasion, there had been several days of rain, and the pathway to the football field for that Friday night's game was muddy. Two parents from the opposing team were negotiating their way to the bleachers when one remarked to the other, regarding the muddy path, "I wonder what MA gets from all their money?" An MA parent, following closely behind, answered, "A good education."

Another of Dr. Johnson's accomplishments was that he had the foresight to have the main gym air conditioned. This has had numerous benefits through the years.

Overall, Dr. Johnson's first few years were exemplary. Then came the infamous basketball coach episode. The story goes like this: Six dads whose sons were not playing as much as the dads thought they should (can you imagine that?) went to Dr. Johnson regarding the basketball coach, Greg Glenn, and the cost of the new library. Allegedly, their sizable pledges hinged on the dismissal of Coach Glenn. His subsequent firing caused an uproar in the athletic department and incurred the wrath of faculty members who were informed about what had happened. The athletic director told Dr. Johnson that the same thing could happen to him. This proved to be an interesting statement.

The upshot was this: we got the library, although some said it was stained with Greg Glenn's blood, and Greg went on to win several state championships in Texas. The irony of the matter is that none of those six boys chose to play basketball the following year.

It was at this point that Dr. Johnson's effectiveness as a leader seemed to decline as a result of what one faculty member described as "his deal with the devil." Complicating the entire library situation was naming co-head librarians for a year, then choosing one of them. There was no way Dr. Johnson was going to win this one. His judgment was seen as a delaying tactic to put off making a decision.

Summing up, Dr. Johnson's first few years were fantastic. His complete body of work proved him to be good for MA. To the end, he was an engaging people person who really cared for others.

Dr. Don Beers, a retired colonel, became our interim Headmaster for one year and did a fantastic job. He, too, had an engaging personality. Dr. Beers was an old-school, teach-them-the-fundamentals-and-hold-their-noses-to-the-grindstone educator who believed in accountability from everyone from the top down, and he accomplished this in a positive manner. This free-from-politics approach was welcomed by a large segment, but his overall philosophy did not go over well with a few of the newer teachers in the Upper School. As with all previous Heads, Dr. Beers's wife was fully supportive, and she did not push herself into the affairs of the school.

When the search for a new Headmaster began, Dr. Beers had already stated that he did not wish to be a candidate. At the urging of the search committee, Dr. Beers allowed himself to become a candidate. Then the most bizarre situation occurred. He was not selected! Everyone I have talked to in the business world as well as in academia said that asking someone to apply was tantamount to offering them the job. To do otherwise was simply unheard of. Yet that is what happened, and in a decision that would have far-reaching effects, Archibald Douglas, a man with no Headmaster experience, was hired. I have seen Dr. Beers's impressive resume and credentials. The mystery of this decision yet remains.

2

MR. DOUGLAS

As new Headmaster, Archibald Douglas seemingly had two main goals: change and diversity. He brought a liberal New England mindset to The Montgomery Academy, which made Dr. Johnson look like a conservative by comparison. He seemed determined to mold MA into his image. He told the faculty that he had the full backing of the trustees, or he would not have accepted the position.

One of his first acts was to assign the faculty to read a book, *Who Moved My Cheese?* It was one of the most one-sided treatments of a subject that I have ever read, and because of that, he lost credibility in my eyes. The premise of the book was that any and all change was good (whether needed or not), and any opposition to change was bad and shortsighted.

Regarding diversity: doubtlessly, MA needed it, but what so many people refused to accept was that reverse discrimination was just as prevalent and just as undesirable as discrimination. It seemed that so many people who preached tolerance were the most intolerant of views opposing their own. I have always felt that the purpose of MA was to provide the finest possible education for youngsters who were truly academically qualified to attend; MA was not a place for social experimentation. Frankly, I really did not care if the school was all white, all black, all Hispanic, or all Asian, for example, as long as every student was held to the same admission standards. To give points on the admission score based on race or ethnicity was just wrong and was discrimination at its worst.

There were some marvelous accomplishments attained during Mr. Douglas's time. There was the beautiful new theater, a much-needed lunchroom overhaul, a commons in the Upper School, and beautification of the school grounds and campus, along with a new soccer pitch and track and field facilities.

To his credit, Mr. Douglas was a very good writer and could express himself well on the written page.

If Mr. Douglas's goals were change and diversification, then his tenure from 2001 to 2009 was most successful. Doubtless, his was the most controversial term between the years 1976 to 2010. At its conclusion, there was deep division among parents, the board, and the faculty. I liken it to a split in a church congregation in which the pastor, in that case, did the honorable thing and, rather than try to stay on, voluntarily resigned, realizing that to fight for his job would only widen the chasm and further injure the church.

A preview of Mr. Douglas's liberal views occurred during his first graduation ceremony. A group of graduating male students decided to make water pistols a part of the ceremony, humiliating MA US Director Peter Trau, while Mr. Douglas stood by and made no move to stop it. The only other time anything like this had ever happened was when some non-MA friends of an MA grad created a disturbance when the graduate's name was called.

Jim Robertson, then US Director, stopped the ceremony and blessed the perpetrators with a grim "try-it-again-and-see-what-happens" stare. That ended it. The audience, used to dignified ceremonies as befitted our school, was shocked at this onstage outrage, except for the parents of a few of the students, who thought their little darlings were "cute."

At the time, the faculty was amazed that Mr. Douglas did not stop the proceedings long enough to put a stop to the shameful behavior. But, as he said afterward, this was being done all over the country, and he saw nothing wrong with it—that is, until the telephones of the board members started ringing off the hook. Well, he then decided it was indeed a bad thing and vowed it would never happen again. In fact, he did take positive steps to insure that no such happenings would again occur at graduation.

We were accustomed to people who were consistent in their professional relationships. Mr. Douglas was anything but. You never knew when you spoke to him what his response would be. At times, he would be quite warm and friendly. Sometimes, he would look at you and grunt; at other times, he would ignore you completely as though you were not even there. A couple of staffers had an interesting and plausible theory for this, but that is not for this book.

In one-on-one meetings with Mr. Douglas, I found him to be cordial, supportive, and professional. That makes his lack of people skills elsewhere quite puzzling

Unfortunately, a number of student regulations and policies were "liberalized." Whether fact or perception, several of them seemed to be for the convenience or preferences of his sons. Adherence to the dress code and hair styling were two examples. Mr. Douglas at least tacitly approved loosening the dress expectations of the faculty. One of the things that attracted me to MA was the professional way in which the faculty members dressed.

Dr. Johnson actually laid the groundwork for relaxing the dress code for faculty when he granted the art teacher permission not to wear a tie in his class, even though John Tatum had worn one every day he taught art and did so without complaint. However, nothing topped one of Mr. Douglas's hires, a new teacher who showed up at a preschool faculty meeting wearing jeans with holes in the knees. People tend to do what they are required to do.

There was a policy in place that prevented designated cash gifts to MA. In other words, I could not give a check to the school specifically to be used for the Middle School girls basketball team. All cash gifts were used for the budget already in place. However, it has been alleged by several very close to the situation that substantial gifts were given and designated to one specific sport within the athletic program with at least the approval of Mr. Douglas and perhaps something much more tangible than just approving other people doing this.

Enforcement of discipline was extremely inconsistent. The virtual ignoring of the dress code was only a symptom. For example, at the conclusion of one year, several seniors pulled a prank, defacing part of the campus. Two of them were caught, but since the others escaped, it was decided that it would not be "fair" to punish just those two, so nothing was done. I hope our law enforcement organizations and court system do not resort to that policy.

Another example: an "A" student with sterling character happened to be riding in the back seat of a car during homecoming week, not knowing the driver was going to play a prank. Yet that unaware girl got the exact same punishment as three members of an athletic team who were busted for smoking pot on a team trip. Whether Mr. Douglas set those punishments or not, I do not know, but he was certainly aware of them and, as Headmaster, approved of them and could have overruled them as he did on some occasions.

In Mr. Douglas's final year, a student was caught violating the athletic department's alcohol and drug policy, which was this student's second offense. Mr. Douglas first agreed to uphold the policy, which incidentally was not instituted by the coaches nor Headmaster, but by the trustees several years previous. But following a visit by the boy's father, Mr. Douglas not only reinstated the athlete but threw out the policy. This was not the first time he had overruled an athletic department disciplinary action.

This flip-flop, of course, subjected MA to the ridicule of the community and of the other private schools, especially in their recruiting. Mr. Douglas's philosophy was, "Boys will be boys." A noted writer, Rick Riley, expressed a sounder philosophy: "Boys will be boys and shame on us as adults for condoning it and allowing it."

It is interesting that every time Mr. Douglas replaced a person in authority, he did so with a female, usually a single woman. The only position of authority at this writing who is a male is the athletic director, and Mr. Douglas tried to hire a female for that job. You can form your own opinion as to this policy. Psychiatrists have an enlightening take on it.

An interesting example of fiscal irresponsibility during the Douglas reign occurred when one student wanted to take a course that we did not offer. So the school paid all the costs and expenses for a former teacher to attend the University of Alabama that summer to be prepared to teach that course, then paid that teacher to teach just one student.

Two of Mr. Douglas's most interesting hires were an Upper School computer teacher and an Upper School science person. The kids said that the new computer person was not well-grounded in computer knowledge and that her main role was to promote tolerance. In fact, they referred to her class as "Tolerance Tech."

The other hire was announced at a faculty meeting prior to the beginning of school one year when Mr. Douglas announced the hiring of a gentleman whose job was to "upgrade the science department and bring it up to the level of the other departments." This to the astonishment of the science department chair who was not informed, much less consulted, on this. A notable bit of information about this new science teacher is that he had a student who was barely passing his other subjects, yet had an average of "96" in this teacher's class, *Conceptual Physics!*

The trustees had decreed a drug testing program for all students and employees. Mr. Douglas was on record as being opposed to any type of drug testing. This science savior announced to his classes that he would not take a drug test. He would quit before being tested, he said. This was obviously open defiance to the board's mandate. You will have to draw your own conclusions as to why. A few days later he told his classes that he had met with Mr. Douglas, and Mr. Douglas had assured him that he had nothing to be concerned about. Interestingly, in spite of the trustees' instructions, the faculty was never tested that year. Mr. Douglas said that he somehow allowed it to "slip through the cracks." The board responded that testing *would* occur the following year. I never saw why anyone would object to being tested unless he or she had something to hide.

Each year, the faculty selects students for individual awards. The year prior to Mr. Douglas's last year, Haley Andreades won all the major subject awards, as she had a 100 average in each course as well as the character award. Mr. Douglas was not pleased. In spite of Haley's hard work to deserve each award she won, Mr. Douglas felt the awards should be spread around. I guess, to be honest, we would have to have called it the "second place award."

Also, prior to Mr. Douglas's arrival, we had always given two character awards in grades five through twelve. After a year in which girls dominated this award, Mr. Douglas decreed that in the future each grade would have to have a boy winner and a girl winner. It did not matter if there might be three guys more deserving than any girl, she would still get an award and two deserving guys would be deprived.

Another occurrence was what I shall call "political preference-gate." During an election, Mr. Douglas sent an e-mail to teachers telling the faculty not to express any political opinions nor display any preferences on campus. Yet he had placed on the school's car a bumper sticker reading, "I am a big blue dot in a red state." Then during the presidential election of 2008, Mr. Douglas started wearing a button promoting his candidate as well as placing a bumper sticker on the same car. When confronted about the hypocrisy, Mr. Douglas had another case of "selective memory" and did not remember the previously mentioned edict. Fortunately, an MA employee had a hard copy of the directive. At any rate, the campaign button along with the bumper stickers disappeared from the MA car, ostensibly at the orders of the trustees.

Then began a series of events some called "the perfect storm" that led to Mr. Douglas's departure. Of course, the alcohol and drug policy had already been abolished. Therefore, when a student government organization from MA attended a convention, it seems a number of students had a big booze party. One student was rushed to the hospital with alcohol poisoning, and the entire group was kicked out of the convention.

Then came the infamous assembly. This involved an outside speaker who promoted gay marriage. No students or parents received any advance notification of this topic, nor was any option given regarding attendance. There are two versions: Mr. Douglas said he knew nothing about the content of the assembly in advance. If he did not, as Headmaster, shouldn't he have? The staff member who set up the assembly said that he twice spoke with Mr. Douglas about it prior to the assembly.

Following this assembly, the water hit the wheel. Parents were outraged. There was more recruiting fodder for competing schools. Instead of being the booze school, then the drug school, we were now portrayed as the gay school. (The reader will have to determine for himself or herself if any of these are a good thing or a bad thing.)

The ability of Mr. Douglas to lead was called into question, so a series of three open meetings was arranged.

I attended the night meeting. It was a hostile environment with a sharply divided audience. I must say Mr. Douglas was magnificent. I do not know if it was acting or not, but it was an Oscar-deserving performance. His sleeves were rolled up, and he tossed his head, used facial expressions, and gestured better than any of the great movie actors. Only he knows if it was sincere or put-on, but again I give him great credit for pulling off one for the ages.

Mr. Douglas sent out a letter addressing the assembly issue, again denying foreknowledge of the event. The staff member who set it up either resigned or was dismissed immediately. In his letter, Mr. Douglas promised a second assembly presenting the opposite viewpoint. Guess what? That second assembly never occurred. I have never understood how a man as obviously intelligent as Mr. Douglas could "forget" important things he was opposed to.

One other example involving the safety of our students must be mentioned. It deals with athletics. In transporting teams in a school minibus, one of our coaches drove at a very high rate of speed. On at least three occasions concerned citizens telephoned the school to report it, twice on one trip from two different states. I can tell you that Dr. Johnson would have taken driving privileges away, if not outright firing the individual. No such thing happened under Mr. Douglas's watch. The athletic director at the time strongly recommended this action, then wrote an official letter to Mr. Douglas stating his position in view of liability.

No one will ever know how close Mr. Douglas came to keeping his position. He had one year remaining on his contract. Speculation is that had it not been for determination on the part of a number of parents to dismiss him, he would have weathered the storm.

After these three open meetings, there was quite a bit of tension and attempts to influence the committee. An Upper School teacher told me that a group of four or five Upper School teachers who supported Mr. Douglas were selected or approved by the director to appear before the board or committee to speak or at least to write letters in support of Mr. Douglas. When this became known, some Upper School teachers, who were against Mr. Douglas, opposed the idea. In the end, neither group was heard in an official capacity.

Regarding the Middle School, I can honestly say that I heard only one Middle School teacher voice approval of Mr. Douglas. The remainder, who made their feelings known, were adamant in their opposition to him.

The situation was rapidly approaching a climax as numerous families, including some prominent and MA legacy families, threatened to withdraw their children if Mr. Douglas was retained.

The MA spin on this was that the withdrawals would be for economic reasons, even though many of them were pursuing enrollment at other private schools. Also, there was the threat to withhold pledges on the new developments at the school.

With attorneys finalizing the details, Mr. Douglas "resigned." It was allegedly the same type of resignation as those of college coaches Tommy Tuberville and Mark Gottfried. That is, they were paid their salary for the remainder of their contract. It would not be the first time MA had paid an administrator not to work, or even a teacher for that matter.

[Readers: If you have an opportunity to be in the Middle School offices area, walk upstairs and look at the portraits of all the Headmasters. Anything jump out at you? I think this represents a microcosm of Mr. Douglas.]

Interestingly, in the summer a year after Mr. Douglas's departure, a former student visited me and asked how the school year went. The student observed that with Mr. Douglas gone there was surely much more discipline and structure.

Mr. Douglas's departure left a divided school community with high passions on both sides. Was he good for MA? It depends upon whom you ask. Time will provide the ultimate answer.

I am deliberately not mentioning any current administrators. History will also judge their tenures. I will just simply say that they are good people currently doing a good job.

Other Administrators

I would like to mention two other former MA administrators. As Middle School director, Diane Blondheim was an outstanding administrator. She had close friends on her faculty, but I never saw any indication of her playing favorites. She was a strict disciplinarian who never avoided a confrontation if one was needed, be it with a student, teacher, or parent. She never hesitated to contact a parent if there was a problem with a student. If a situation occurred involving an individual teacher, she met individually with that teacher. She was quick to praise when justified. When a child was sent to her for disciplinary reasons, the child did not look forward to the trip. The school is much better for her having been there.

Dr. Jim Robinson was an Upper School director who preached and practiced strict accountability. Although he and I disagreed on some philosophical beliefs, I respected the man highly. Playing politics was not in his nature. It did not matter if a family was a heavy contributor or a non-contributor: they were treated the same, as were their children if a problem arose. For example, he did not just preach adherence to the dress code, he personally attended to it, keeping a razor in his desk for unshaven boys and a frumpy dress for girls whose skirts were too short. He was good for the school and its image.

If asked to rank the top MA Headmasters for their overall effectiveness in upholding the standards of MA, based upon their complete term of service and body of work, I'd do so as follows:

1. Wade Segrest
2. Dr. Donald Beers
3. Dr. Emerson Johnson
4. Robin Byrd

Although I stated that current administrators would not be mentioned in this work, I must bring to light two developments that merit noting. Not only does she support drug testing, but Vivian Barfoot actually helped the physical education teachers administer the tests in 2010. Dave Farace has made a very impressive early impression. There are many fences to mend and a lot of serious wounds to heal, but he is doing an excellent job at this. This is a man who is interested in the culture of The Montgomery Academy and is embracing it, rather than trying to mold the school in his own image. Also, following some undesirable behavior on the part of some of our fans at the first football game of 2010, Dave Farace notified all the parents of football players at MA that this would not be tolerated. Isn't it *great* to see leaders being proactive and positive and working to restore MA's image and returning our school to the standards and values upon which it was created?

I will close this section with a curious fact: during my thirty-five years at MA, when a Headmaster was replaced, it was never with a person who was a Headmaster at another school at the time.

3

FACULTY

When I came to MA, I was honored to be part of a faculty that included master teachers like Gene Crouch, English; Marg Dubina, English; Mary Roten, math; J. O. Lawrence, physics; and Mary Carlson, chemistry. R. B. Roberts, history, joined the faculty the same time as I. There were many more legendary teachers in grades K–6 who I did not get to know as well due to my teaching assignments and the fact that my son started in the seventh grade. Mrs. Berry was the librarian and in a unique situation. Her husband was a beekeeper, while her daughter, Catherine, was very allergic to bee stings.

The teachers I just named did not cut any corners. Students earned their grades by demonstrating their knowledge of the subject. They did not believe in "frills" that would add points to bring a student's grade up to insure a passing grade, especially if the work did not reflect a student's mastery of the subject. Through the years, The Montgomery Academy has been the beneficiary of the wisdom of many other teachers such as these.

Mr. Crouch, with whom I had taught at Goodwyn Junior High School, was a stern taskmaster. I felt I became a much better student of English as I spent many an hour with my son reviewing him for his tests and quizzes.

Mr. Lawrence had a unique teaching style. Any day you came into his physics classroom, you were expected to be prepared for a major test covering all the new material since the previous test. He never announced a physics test in advance. Can you imagine the outcry against such a demanding of excellence today?

Mrs. Roten was known as "Mrs. Smokin' Roten," because it was said that as she explained and wrote the solution to a math problem on the board with her right hand, her left hand followed quickly behind with an eraser. True or not, she was excellent.

Mr. Roberts had an unusual way of teaching. He stressed "thinking." He allowed no clock in his room. His students were not allowed to take notes in class. He would frequently tell the MA students historical untruths and then ask a question about this on a test and expect them to get it right. He expected them to think and ferret out the correct information.

Mr. Roberts's philosophy was to "let the chips lie where they fell" gradewise. If a student had a final grade of 69, that student failed. A 70 was a pass, not a 69. He also had a stool in a corner of his classroom and an old-fashioned, tall pointed cap with the word *DUNCE* printed in large letters down one side. Numerous students spent a class period sitting on that stool and wearing that cap.

Mr. Roberts, to put it mildly, did not like administrative bureaucracy. He frequently threatened "to resign right now." I think I hurt his feelings one day when I replied that we could both quit on the spot and would not cause a ripple.

Former football coach Spence McCracken joined the faculty with classroom responsibilities in history. Part of history was the previous Friday night's football game, and students should certainly better know that score on a history test.

Mrs. Bryant Allen became the new librarian. Woe be to the unfortunate student who dared to lean back in his or her chair. It was said that Mrs. Allen believed that books were not made to be checked out and read, but rather to look pretty sitting on the shelves.

Ken Dyess was truly a jack-of-all-trades. At various times, he served as math teacher, assistant Headmaster, Middle School director, and interim Headmaster. He was an excellent teacher, beloved by his students.

There is a story that one of the school secretaries threatened to turn Mr. Dyess in to the Honor Council for working the students' problems for them on tests.

Mr. Dyess did me a huge favor when he steered me in the direction of the Middle School when I had to make a decision between it and teaching in the Upper School. You could always tell from a distance when Mr. Dyess had told a joke. He would be talking and burst out laughing, while those around him would look at each other with puzzled looks on their faces.

In a meeting of the POA, there was a particularly boring moderator. Mr. Dyess slipped me a note that said, "I think I may expire."

When Mrs. Carlson left, a new chemistry teacher joined the faculty. He only stayed for a year, but it was memorable. To say that his classes were unruly would be a vast understatement. My room adjoined his, and at times it seemed the walls would vibrate. One day, he lost patience and told the class that he was going to count to three and that they had better be quiet. He started, "One," and the entire class joined in, yelling, "Two, three!"

The teacher got his revenge on Class Day. At that time, the seniors took their exams one week early, so the following week on Class Day, they would spoof the faculty at a special assembly the first thing in the morning. Then they would go to the lake for the remainder of the day.

On this particular day, the seniors decided to park crossways in the parking lot, with each of their cars taking up three of the limited parking spaces. The chemistry teacher, arriving late, could not find anywhere to park and thus had to park at the adjoining service station and walk to the campus. Rather than attend the festivities, he let the air out of all four tires of each of the seniors' cars. So much for the lake trip.

Since the seniors had taken their exams early, the senior trip at that time was under the supervision of the school. At some point, the school wised up and got out of that responsibility. When my son was a senior, Mr. Roberts was there early on the morning of their departure, handing out graded exam papers. As soon as the bus got off campus and onto Vaughn Road, papers came flying out of the bus windows.

The following year, yet another chemistry teacher joined the faculty. She was an excellent teacher but spent considerable class time extolling the exploits of her water-skiing son. In fact, one student, who had gotten out of her sickbed to come to an exam review, complained to the Headmaster when a good bit of the review time was spent talking about the teacher's son. The Headmaster then forbade the teacher from uttering her son's name in class, so she then referred to him as "You Know Who."

This reminds me of one of my favorite mantras: "Never talk about your children, grandchildren, team you coach, etc., unless you are first asked, then keep it mercifully brief. Also remember in your conversations, that most people do not share your passions and interests and are bored hearing about them."

In this same teacher's class, a couple of innovative young men procured a remote to the VCR that looked exactly like the one the teacher used. One day when she attempted to show a video, they confounded matters with their remote. When she would press "start," they would secretly press "stop." When she attempted to "rewind," they would hit "fast forward." This went on for several minutes before mercy was declared.

One teacher certainly believed in the honor system. While her class was working on page one of an exam, she would be in the teachers' workroom copying page two.

Ever hear of a football coach who taught art? Well, we had one. John Tatum brought his unique talents to MA and was excellent in both areas.

English teacher Sue Scalf had a great way of curing "test-itis," a malady that seemed to keep some children home ill on test days. She gave all her make-up tests only on Friday afternoon after school. Her students had the lowest incidences of illness on test days of any faculty member.

An interesting individual was a coach/teacher in the history department. He loved to sit in a swing during his planning period and talk to himself. He frequently gave his students unusual challenges, such as swallowing a live goldfish.

I will never forget a young English teacher who wore argyle socks. When his class would misbehave, which was frequently, he would leave the class to go sit in his car and pout.

A Korean War veteran, Bob Hayes, was at one time an excellent physics teacher at MA. He had an unusual way of beginning the year. He would announce on the first day that the class was seven days behind, and usually he threw a piece of chalk at someone.

In 1988, there was an unusual addition to the math faculty—former Headmaster Wade Segrest returned as a math instructor. He was just as excellent in the classroom as he had been as an administrator. He was to return several years later and finish out the year for a teacher who resigned before the year was out.

In 1992, Sydney Davis joined the faculty as drama teacher. On her first day on the job, in the afternoon session of the first day of faculty meetings, Sydney stood and went around the room, identifying each teacher by name. This was simply astounding, especially to myself, as I have trouble remembering a name five minutes after an introduction.

Jay Rye joined the faculty as speech/history teacher. As forensics coach, Jay's teams have won so many state championships and he has sent so many of his students to college forensic teams that I refer to him as "Bear," as in "Bear" Bryant.

Mark Smucker (yep, same family) was hired as eighth-grade science teacher. This story was not told until after he left, but several students confirmed that if they bought a techno music (the type of music that sounds like two garbage can lids being banged together) recording he made, he would give them five extra points.

The following year, Laura Spivey, an outstanding math teacher, joined the Middle School faculty. She patiently guided me, kicking and screaming, into the complexities of the computer age. In three years, I was actually able to turn on a computer by myself, for which Laura gave me a giant Hershey bar.

Irony of ironies, a student won as a prize, a computer, and gave it to me. This was the first computer in the science department, and Jennifer Grant and I shared it. She obviously had a lot more stored on it than I did. Sadly, one day, the computer died, and everything on it was lost. We had a very solemn memorial ceremony and buried the hard drive on school grounds.

A number of former students have returned to MA in some capacity during my time at the school. I'm sure that I will miss mentioning some, but the first, I believe, during my time, was Lisa Saylor Lee as drama teacher.

A former MA Hitchcock Award winner, Robert Johnson came on board as a math teacher.

In 1995, two more MA alums joined the faculty—J. B. Copeland, math, and Leslie Little, physical education.

Leslie is a delightful person, and there are two humorous stories about her. She speaks rather loudly. In fact, a former coach said she must have been raised in a helicopter. Also, as a coach driving her teams in a cheese wagon, the school minibus, Leslie is said never to have seen a pothole or curb that she did not like and that, if she missed one, she would turn around and go back and hit it.

Another hire was mysteriously added to the faculty. She gave us an international flavor, but there was a problem. She spoke very little English, so an additional teacher had to be paid to go into the classroom to interpret.

This was also the year that Jennifer Grant became the eighth-grade science teacher. Jennifer is a truly dedicated professional with a heart of gold. She and I took care of many litters of stray kittens, not to mention the baby squirrels, birds, and other creatures that found their way to our area.

A number of years ago, an outstanding English teacher, Jerry Pickett, once told a particularly obnoxious student, "Okay, 'Billy,' we have all seen you, so you can now crawl back under your rock." Obviously, those were the "good old days" before political correctness and sensitivity and of being offended.

In January 1997, former MA student Caroline Sease was hired to rescue the seventh-grade English class. No need to go into the details, but it was a mess. Caroline had to bring the students up to speed academically and establish order, both of which she did most efficiently.

Larry Vinson, a computer guru if there ever was one, was hired to head and upgrade the technology department. More about Larry later.

In 1997, I decided to relinquish my post as chairman of the science department. I did not feel I was qualified to lead the department into the twenty-first century considering all the technological advances coming our way.

In 1999, former MA student and number-one player on the MA tennis team Tanner Rees became an extended day faculty member.

Tanner's dad, Dave, gave me one of my most prized possessions—one of Casey Stengel's walking sticks. To complete the cycle, Tanner later married Matt Munson, a relative of Thurman Munson. Dave was a huge Red Sox fan. That same year, Whitney Wills, another former MA athlete, joined the English faculty.

In the early 2000s, two more MA alums joined the faculty: William Carroll and John McWilliams. In 2007 another alum, Philip Sellers, came.

Again, I must apologize to the Lower School teachers and somewhat to those in the Upper School for failing to give them their due recognition, but The Montgomery Academy is actually three separate entities, and those of us in the Middle School seldom saw or talked with the teachers in the other divisions.

I do wish to pay tribute to those Middle School teachers I have not previously mentioned and who were still on the faculty at the conclusion of the 2009–2010 year. They are dedicated professionals with whom I am honored to have worked. They are Scott Bowman, Amanda Townsend, Pam Gilpin, Wendy Hamil, Susan Harris, Debbie Kranzusch, Gene Johnson, Lura McMillan, Wilfredo Navidad, Teresa Pittman, Carol Quallio, Susan Riley, Betty Saunders, Kitty Sheehan, Damion Womack, Dale Thomas, and Denise Tinney. I hope I did not leave anyone out. Some I have mentioned previously or will mention in another section.

Amanda and Scott deserve special mention. They both teach activities-centered classes, which could easily turn into a zoo, but both are excellent classroom managers. This is greatly appreciated by those of us who teach or taught next to them.

In addition to being an excellent Latin teacher, Teresa Pittman is a true professional. She will always volunteer when help is needed. Teresa also teaches a class called interpersonal relations. She frequently takes this group out into disadvantaged neighborhoods to render aid.

A special commendation and thanks is due to Jerry Pickett for never losing it while correcting my endless grammatical errors on all the communiqués with parents.

Among the Lower School teachers who "returned home" to teach and staff members are Allison Finklea, Joscie Bolton, Jane Crenshaw, Carolyn East, Allison Chandler, Jodi Chesnutt, Beth Eskridge,

Megan German, Meribeth Pyper Parrish, Ashlee Hooper, Margaret Beck, Ellen Bell, Frances Smith, and Rebecca Hollingsworth.

This is as good a place as any to point out that at MA, unlike public schools, teachers do not have tenure. With tenure, after you have taught for three years, it is almost impossible to be fired. As the governor of New Jersey recently stated, "If you are still breathing, you are still getting paid."

At MA, teachers have to prove themselves each year. This certainly assures the parents and students of quality teachers. Also, there is no salary schedule; therefore, the Headmaster, operating within the constraints of the budget, determines each individual teacher's worth. A number of teachers would negotiate with the Headmaster. I never did. I always signed my contract for what was offered. I felt I was fortunate to be there and felt I was being treated and paid fairly. If I could have afforded it, I would have paid the school to teach there.

I have related to you some amusing anecdotes about MA teachers. No doubt there are many more that could be told on me. With the misadventures, it can be safely said that the faculty at MA is as fine as can be found. This is proven by our record of college acceptances for our graduates.

I will relate one tale on myself. A few years ago, I informed Mrs. Pickett that I had an appointment with a member of my board of physicians early one morning and might be late to my first period class. Coach David Bethea was going to cover for me. Well, David forgot to cover and Middle School director Jerry Pickett forgot also. Since I regularly got to school by 6:30 each morning, when I had not appeared in my room by 8:10, one of the students reported it to the office.

Obviously thinking I was dead in my bed, Mrs. Pickett called the athletic director Anthony McCall to see if he would go to my house to check on me. Coach McCall enlisted maintenance supervisor Steve German to go with him. I keep a golf club by my back door. I carry it with me to ward off the varmints when I go running, er, jogging—walking. Get the picture now?

My backdoor neighbor looks out her window and sees this tall black guy and this middle-aged white guy hoisting a golf club looking in my back window. She grabs her telephone and starts to dial 911 when they drive off. Meanwhile, Mrs. Anderson sees me walking up the sidewalk and informs Mrs. Pickett that Mr. Jones or his ghost is at school. That is what happens when you get ancient. If you are not where you are supposed to be, people automatically think you are extinct and have assumed room temperature

Obviously, over thirty-five years, there are changes in personnel. Teachers resign or retire. A few are fired, some fail to have their contracts renewed, and a few depart under mysterious circumstances.

This section would not be complete without relating the four most bizarre incidents involving faculty. In my very first year at MA, a fifth-grade teacher was arrested on campus for shooting his *boyfriend* the previous night. This was thirty-five years ago.

Another incident occurred when an administrator walked in on a female teacher and a male student in an inappropriate situation. Not *that* inappropriate, but inappropriate nonetheless.

A most unprofessional, unethical happening occurred when a teacher showed a student how to get into the faculty computer grading system and change her grade in another teacher's class, which the student did.

The most despicable, disgusting incident that occurred in my thirty-five years happened just a few years ago. The dad of an Upper School student who was serving in Afghanistan and putting his life on the line each day sent some pictures to his daughter. She was showing them to another student in the hall between classes when this "teacher" approached and inquired as to the pictures. When the student told her, this individual launched into an antiwar tirade that reduced the student to tears. I do not know what is most shameful, the actions of this "teacher" or the fact that she was not fired on the spot.

Needless to say, none of these teachers is still employed at MA.

Some staff members deserve special recognition for various reasons. Former longtime business manager Jane Renfro worked incredible hours and did the work of three people. Joyce Sweatt, legendary secretary for many years, seemed to be the glue that held the school together.

We have had many heads of maintenance. I guess the least popular was a tall guy with an incredibly bad temper. Two MA coaches almost got into fistfights with him on separate occasions.

Retired colonel Steve German brought to fruition a list of innovative ideas. Someone remarked that where else but at MA would you find a retired colonel mowing the grass. Steve was not a delegator who stayed in an air-conditioned office all day. He could be found on the "front lines" doing the grub work. The colonel was a strict disciplinarian, and a few of, shall we say, the less well-behaved students did not care for him because he did not subscribe to the prevailing theory of the time, "Boys will be boys," nor did he care who anyone's parents were.

Although this book as a rule does not comment on current personnel, an exception must be made for two stalwarts. Clayton Dunavant is a jewel. His work ethic is unparalleled, and he does it with a great attitude. I really appreciate this man. I must tell one anecdote. Clayton literally tore down a wall in the school lunchroom, knowing he would have to repair it, to rescue three baby kittens that had fallen in between two walls and were starving. These have grown into fine cat-hood now and belong to Coach Lowe and Abi Capouya.

I do not have the words to describe how much I appreciate and am indebted to Connie Johnson, who is the school registrar but carries a lot of other unofficial titles. Without her always-more-than-willing-to-help attitude, I would have stayed at least five years behind. I frequently made the statement that if Connie left, I would be right behind her. MA is a far better place because of Clayton and Connie.

I always found the "upstairs ladies," Carolyn Bryan, her staff, and the "downstairs ladies" as well to always be extremely helpful and considerate.

One recent anecdote. As you may know, there is no protection from the elements in going between the Upper and Middle School building. During a downpour, some Middle School students slogged over to the Upper School for a class. When they arrived, they were informed that they needed their workbooks. So they braved the deluge and went back to their lockers. Then, thoroughly drenched by now, they dashed through the flood again. Guess what? They never used their workbooks that day.

At midyear, a year and a half prior to my retirement, I did a self-evaluation of my teaching and became extremely disgusted at how much I had allowed the standards in my class over the years to gradually deteriorate so that the less qualified and, perhaps, unqualified students, who in previous years would probably not have been admitted, would pass. A passing grade in my class did not mean nearly as much as it used to, and the bright students, for whom the school was conceived, were not being sufficiently challenged.

So I informed my director and the other seventh-grade teachers that I was going back to the way I taught and tested fifteen years ago. Class grades went down except for those students for whom the school was created, and I ended up with more failures for the year than I had had in the previous twenty years combined.

I am not proud of having those failures, and I feel very badly for those kids, but I could sleep at night knowing that I was again providing an MA-type of education. Incidentally, those same students also failed two other subjects. Significantly, the students who had high grades maintained them, so this certainly does not take away from the achievement of the good students in previous years as, doubtless, they too would have maintained their level of achievement.

I am extremely happy that Denise Tinney will now be teaching seventh-grade science. She is an excellent teacher who will maintain high academic standards and will hold the students accountable.

I thoroughly enjoyed my thirty-five years at MA, which was about half my lifetime, and I felt privileged to be allowed to teach at such a fine school with such a distinguished faculty. For thirty-five years, each day as I drove to work, including my last day, I sang (not very well) because I was so happy and looking forward to teaching the youngsters. Rare was the day when I did not look forward to going to work, and rarely did those few days have anything to do with a student. I love the kids, I loved teaching, and I cherish the relationships of those professionals with whom I was honored to work.

If I was enjoying what I was doing, why did I retire? There would be two reasons.

First, I have seen teachers, administrators, coaches, athletes, ministers, entertainers, and others stay on well past their effectiveness and become objects of pity and ridicule, and most of the time, they do not even realize it. For me to stay beyond my time would not be fair to the students, the parents, or the school.

The second reason reminds me of a previous MA employee who retired saying she was "parented out, tired of raising parents." Well, I was "technological-ed out." I had to be dragged kicking and screaming into the computer age. My late father-in-law was worse than I. His view was, "Now, I am all for progress, *but*—"

Seems like every time that I started to feel comfortable with the computer, there would be the inevitable upgrades, changes, and additional things we had to do on the computer. I think I was the only teacher left in the Middle School who still used a "dumb board." I have no idea what an e-pods are, or what a tweetsie is. To me, texting refers to reading a school textbook and blackberries are something you make cobblers from, and what in the world is a "Lady Goo Goo"?

Now, lest I be misunderstood, technology is wonderful, and MA is doing what needs to be done to prepare our students for the future. The school is doing at least as well, if not better than any other school in the area. I just decided, knowing that I did not have nearly as many years left as I had already lived, that I preferred spending that time with other priorities: First Baptist Church, BAMA sports, the New York Yankees, Mayberry, and my beloved cats.

My ten-year-old cats are Bootfeet Jones, Blackie the Cat, and Fat Brownie (although my brother-in-law wanted me to name them Inky, Dinky, and Stinky), along with two strays that have adopted me as their human, Stripes and Goldie. Goldie is deaf, crippled, and, I believe, one of the two cats that Noah took on the ark. Blackie the Cat has developed a fondness for Reddi-wip. One day, I mistakenly bought another brand, and he turned up his nose at it. I informed him that he was either going to lap that or else … I would go to the store and buy some Reddi-Wip, which I did.

Then there is my pet cardinal, "Mr. Cardinal." He greets me from a tree limb every afternoon when I arrive at home with a "tweet" for his bird food. One day, I ignored him and started toward the house. He flew to a closer limb and tweeted more loudly. As I started to unlock the back door, he actually flew under the carport roof with a very loud *tweeeeet!*

In other words, I am going to be doing the things I really love and enjoy, rather than spending the time continually upgrading and staying behind. That too would have been so unfair to our students. My son gave me a sponge-rubber hammer to use to take out my frustrations on my home computer.

I must pay tribute to Larry and Doc, the computer wizards, who were so kind in giving me all the support they could. They both have the patience of Job, and they earned much more than their salary just trying to guide me. Others that helped me so much in this area and that I really appreciate are Connie (can't help but mention her again), Denise, Jennifer, Teresa, and Laura. Also, thanks to Mirenda Tatum and Carolyn Pyper for a lot of AV assistance.

Accolades must be given to Evelyn Anderson and Rolanda Woods, the two ever-patient, ever-cheerful Middle School secretaries.

One of the few things I will not miss is adhering to this age of sensitivity and political correctness. Terry Harrington stated that tact is for those not intelligent enough to use sarcasm. I grew up with sarcasm. The way we showed affection for each other was by cutting each other down. If someone did not "dis" us, we worried that he or she did not like us. It never seemed to bother our self-esteem. Most of my teaching career was spent this way. The kids and I used to love to banter with each other in a good-natured manner. Lord have mercy. If you did this today, the wrath of the universe would descend upon you.

I have adapted so much over the years that I might not even recognize myself. But in my heart, I am still old school and still believe in the values and standards of "the old days."

The beginning Of the 2010–2011 school year was the first in sixty-five years that I had not been in a classroom as a teacher or student, albeit the starting date was now about one month earlier than the date of September 11, 1944, when I started first grade.

For all of these funny, sad, not-so-good, and a couple of despicable actions that have taken place at MA, most faculty have literally gone way beyond the call of duty for students. I cannot imagine a more caring, loving, and supportive group of teachers anywhere. I say to parents, you may not realize how fortunate and blessed you are to have had your most precious possessions, your children, under the watchful care of these dedicated, truly professional educators.

31

Someone said, "The biggest mistake made by teachers is spending too much time with negative children. We should concentrate our time and efforts with the students who are displaying the behavior, attitude, and effort we want."

To faculty and staff, a final *thank you* to each of you who continue to make The Montgomery Academy a great school and for all you did to help me and to make my stay such an overwhelmingly pleasant experience.

MA Cats

MA has been the home of three resident cats. The first, years ago, was a huge cat that was adopted by Mr. Roberts who named him Socrates. Mr. Roberts, at the suggestion of the Headmaster, eventually took Socrates home to live with him.

We then had, at separate times, two dogs named Barney and Tung Su that visited occasionally. They either followed or were brought by their owners. They were never official residents of MA, as they lived elsewhere.

A tiny ball of fur appeared in the grass between the seventh- and eighth-grade wing and the Headmaster's office. No one ever figured out where the cat came from. Naturally, I started feeding him. He was so wild and terrified that he lived in the bushes under the Headmaster's office. I would put some food down and leave it. After five or so minutes, he would dash out, gobble it down, and rush back into his hiding place. In a few weeks, he allowed me to begin petting him, but he remained a one-person cat until he figured things out. An MA coed named him MAC, for Montgomery Academy Cat.

MAC became a fixture at MA. He had Dr. Johnson's approval, as he was a goodwill ambassador who frequently greeted visitors and prospective parents and could be seen sitting on a child's lap in the Jenny Garden.

When the weather was nice, and the door to my class was open, MAC would sometimes walk in and sit in on the class or, if he was in his politicking mood, find his way to a student's lap. He liked to think that when he was in the class that he raised the overall intelligence level.

He became the ultimate con artist. He would be waiting for me every morning in the parking lot and lead me to his food dish. But he was careful not to let others know he had been fed. There were about four other teachers that he would meet every morning, meowing pitifully, as though he had not eaten in days, and con another feeding out of them. He loved to roam the roof of the breezeway.

MAC spent eight happy years making others happy. He was found one morning lying close to the gym. No marks on him, so the hope was that he passed on quickly and painlessly and is now happily roaming the grounds of that Big Schoolhouse up in the sky. He has a plaque in a flower garden on the grounds of MA.

The current reigning feline is the female version of MAC, Maxine. Maxine is the mother of the three kittens that Mr. Dunavant rescued. She, like her predecessor, just appeared, this time with dependents. She is a beautiful animal, but very shy. She has reached the point of loving to be petted when I would feed her.

Maxine never showed herself until late every afternoon, until, on my very last morning as a teacher at MA, Maxine was waiting for me at my classroom door when I arrived that morning. It would seem as though she was there to tell me goodbye. Figure this one out if you can.

My worry with Maxine is that if she is on the roof when it is feeding time, she will jump off the roof onto the ground. One of these days, she is going to break. Just as I am the Montgomery branch of Stray Cats Shelter, Mr. Vinson is the Prattville branch, and upon my retirement, he graciously consented to be Maxine's caretaker. She is in excellent hands.

4

STUDENTS

A fifth grader approached me on a breezeway and asked, "Are you God?"

I swelled up, preened my feathers, and replied, "Well, ah, no."

The kid responded, "You are as old as He is."

When Findley Frazer raised his hand in class, I called on him, and he asked, "Mr. Jones, is it true that you were on the ark?" I replied that I certainly was *not!* He then asked, "Then why did you not drown with the rest of them?"

That is okay, Findley, your sister, Bowie, told me that when there was a tornado warning, the housekeeper always sent you outside to look for it. I must admit that when I was the age of the current seventh graders, the Dead Sea was just starting to feel a little sick and the Big Dipper was just a little cup.

Now you see, these two episodes are the types of humor I love. It was good-natured, and the students knew where the line was. I have always believed that people who could not laugh at themselves were not pleasant to be around for very long.

This section on MA students is going to be largely anecdotal. I'll use names when people already know about them.

When studying genetics and how we get our traits, a young lady raised her hand and asked, "Can you inherit traits from your uncle?" That broke up the class.

One morning a seventh grader entered my room bursting out in laughter. I asked her what was so funny. She said that her mother was so busy fussing at her and her siblings that she forgot to raise the door to the garage and backed the brand new SUV right into it.

We have another mother who *twice* has driven away from a service station dragging the pop-off gasoline hose all the way home.

Several years ago, close to the end of the school year, a student who had not made above an 84 all year asked if she was going to be exempt from the exam.

At the opposite end of the spectrum, a student who made an A on his exam texted his friends, "Mr. Jones must have made a mistake."

This past year was accreditation year, and the visiting team was standing in the courtyard. A seventh grader walked up to me, pointed to them, and whispered conspiratorially to me, "Those are the inspectors."

Several years ago, there was a third grader who absolutely would not be quiet, even if you sprayed him with Ritalin. Our innovative third-grade teacher stuffed a rolled-up sock in his mouth.

Then we had the brave male student who started out the year dating the oldest of three sisters. By midyear, he was dating the middle one, and by spring he wanted to go out with the eighth-grade sister. I'll bet there were some interesting dinner conversations in that home. That is topped though by an MA coed who had a date with an MA guy but told him she had to be home by ten o'clock for some reason. The reason was that she had a date with his brother at ten-thirty. When both brothers found out, they had a brawling fistfight in their home.

An MA senior was smitten by an MA seventh grader. He put on his best suit and tie and drove to the home of the fair young maiden to ask her parents' permission to take her out. Thankfully, they declined his offer.

An enterprising young lady got the teacher who was perceived to be the harder of the two that taught a course. She went to the office and said that she wanted to take an elective that was offered during that class period. That meant she got the other teacher. Next day, she went in and dropped the elective, thus keeping the "easier" teacher.

One student who was not so enterprising had not done his report for Mrs. Grant. So he borrowed another student's report, made a photocopy of it, and turned in the photocopy! Duh!

Wade Segrest and I bought a "lifetime" pen from Mary Catherine Memory. Mine is still alive and working.

Each year, when the school photographer came, he gave everyone a nickname. He always called me Orville Redenbacher (the old one, the father, the ugliest man ever born). Even after he was *dead!* He referred to a very cute, slightly plump little third-grade girl as Marshmallow. She cried the rest of the day, and they never got her picture taken that day.

There were two female basketball players who were each called the Black Hole because when the ball went to them, it was not coming back. It was going to be launched in the general direction of the goal. Good thing they played in different years or there would have to have been two basketballs. Actually, I may need to add a third player to the list, a young lady who very recently in a game had the ball on the foul line with her back to the basket. She was surrounded by three defenders. Did that deter her? Ha! She merely threw the ball back over her head in the general direction of the basket. Even her father said she had never seen a shot she did not like.

I had the unique experience of coaching against a former student, Craig Bowman, who coached Middle School girls at St. James. Craig's dad and I have been buddies for a long time. Craig and Glenn Sylvest were teammates at MA. I would not want to be the judge of a contest between these two to see whose voice "carried" the best. The first time I sat on the bench with Glenn, speaking in *his* normal voice, voicing his opinion to an official, I almost went through the ceiling, thought I would have a heart attack, and was lucky I did not have to change my underwear.

Several years ago, a student was standing on the sidewalk when the fifth graders returned from PE in the gym. He whispered to several of them, "Hey, you want to buy some drugs," as he held out an aspirin. They went sprinting to the classroom to tell the teacher. A few days later, as fate would have it, he happened to be in the same area when they were returning from lunch. They quickly pointed him out to their teacher who hauled the unfortunate one to the office. It took some effort to convince the Headmaster that the student was joking. Even so, he received some undesired punishment.

When Margaret Peddy was in my room, her mom could flat make fudge, of which I was the happy recipient several times.

Several years later, when Margaret's niece Katherine made the Middle School girls basketball team that I was coaching, she told her aunt that she had made the team. When Margaret asked and was told who the coach was, her response was, "Old Mr. Jones? *Old, Mr. Jones!*" To complete the story, when Margaret's daughter, Mary Margaret, was in my class, she assumed the role of "Official Mr. Jones's Necktie Critic," critiquing whatever tie I wore each day. She was good at it.

Speaking of fudge, one young lady brought me fudge several times, but you had to use a straw and drink it. She could never master the technique of getting it to solidify.

I did not know that Leigh Morris was a gymnast. One morning, before school started, several seventh graders said, "Mr. Jones, look what Leigh can do." Leigh, standing on a wooden floor, no padding, did a standing forward flip, landing on her feet!

When Josie Haas finished her sentence of being taught by me, her mom baked a pound cake for her to take to me the next day. But Josie left it sitting on the kitchen table. Big brother, Bob, came in, saw it there, and proceeded to sit down and eat half of it.

Bob also referred to his girlfriend as Whale Tail. Ouch! Where was political correctness and sensitivity?

Elizabeth Capell got out of the car one morning before school, and as she was walking up to her circle of friends, among many other mingling students, her dad got out of the car and shouted, "Elizabeth, remember to take care of that dress today! We have to carry it back to Arrow Rents after school."

David Morris had an uncle who was a hypnotist. He came to my class one day and hypnotized three students. While hypnotized, Catherine Berry could not uncross her arms. Beth Themes could not close her mouth and stood there with a "duh" expression on her face, and Wanda Snowden could not remember her last name. He brought each of them out of it with key words, but he had to rehypnotize Catherine because her shoulder muscles had tightened so from crossing her arms so tightly.

Another treat, I believe the same year, was when the wife of my pastor at the time, who was a graphoanalyst, analyzed the handwriting of a number of students. Fortunately, she did not find any master criminals in the group.

Mr. Kilton, a math teacher, was the consummate gentleman, but entirely too trusting. A student sat in the back of class playing a new handheld football game that was the rage at the time. When asked by Mr. Kilton what he was doing, the student replied that it was one of those new math calculators. Mr. Kilton believed him, and class continued as did one football game.

Just recently, an administrator heard all sorts of commotion coming from the classroom right above his office. When he went up to investigate, he found the teacher sitting at his desk, while all the students' desks had been pushed aside and a rousing game of soccer was being played in the classroom. The teacher's comment was, "Oh, did we disturb you?"

Katherine Bond (1977–1978) wrote the school anthem, "Soar, Eagles, Soar."

David Bethea served as varsity boys basketball coach at one time. In a tournament game at what is now the Tine Davis Gym, two players who were sitting at the end of the bench, literally and figuratively, had a pizza delivered to them at the bench during the game. Needless to say, their days as questionable basketball players were numbered.

Peggy Bloodworth came to MA in the Upper School. She was a vocalist of considerable talent who recorded a cassette (for those of you who are not old enough, this was the forerunner of CDs) of which I am the proud owner of a copy.

Ginger Anyway was in the same class with Peggy. Ginger was (and still is) a beautiful young lady with a fair complexion and could probably turn redder than anyone when she was embarrassed.

Allison Finklea was another all-American girl. Allison was a cheerleader but had a bad knee. The football team's quarterback was in the same class and, like all quarterbacks should, had a *lot* of confidence in himself, to put it mildly. One day, everyone had finished up their biology lab, and Allison told the QB that she could beat him in a race. He was insulted at the mere suggestion, so we went out on the football field for a 40-yard race. Allison, bad knee and all, beat him by two steps!

Another quarterback and I had a very close encounter—too close. I was taking up money for a varsity football game between the gym and the classroom building several years ago, before all the parking lots. My ancient Plymouth Valiant was parked on the curb on Vaughn Road. The quarterback had forgotten his jersey of all things, so he drove home to get it. A few minutes later, there was a loud crash. The QB had collided with my car. He parked and took off running for the football field. Guess he must have feared the football coach more than he did the law.

There was a student who whined so much about the way his papers were graded that Mr. Dyess finally told him that he was not putting up with his griping any longer and that he could just grade his own papers and determine his own grade.

Two guys were quite perplexing. They were very bright but were so afraid their parents would find out, they deliberately missed questions on tests. They would always make Bs.

My first year, Marc Tyson was in the class. He is Coach Bryant's grandson and a very nice, smart young man and student. He did a great imitation of Fonzie of *Happy Days*.

Among other "names" I have taught are the sons of Governor James and Attorney General Graddick. Also, I taught Congressman Artur Davis.

I called an absent student's home to give an assignment and a very high-pitched voice answered. I asked, "Mrs. Smith?"

And the voice replied, "This is *Mr.* Smith!" Bet I was not the only one to make that mistake.

We had a device that measured muscle strength. Gaylon Thackston was the strongest student in the class. The second strongest was a girl!

Many years ago, three of our cheerleaders were going to the movie in Cloverdale. As they walked down that dark sidewalk between what was then Cloverdale Junior High School and Sinclairs, they were accosted by two guys. Two of the cheerleaders took off running and screaming. The third stuck around and beat the pickle juice out of both of them.

I still have two framed portraits done by Chelse Beck—one of the BAMA Elephant, the other of the MA Eagle.

One student was not invited back for a following year. She showed up anyway. The office thought they had misplaced her schedule card and made her one. She wound up graduating from MA.

I've had a number of "trio students"—threesomes that hung around together. One such group was Beth Beshear, Bowie Frazier, and Kristen Hatcher. There is a great photo of them in one of their kitchens making cookies.

Clinton Segrest is the son of Headmaster Wade Segrest. One day I met him in the breezeway and absent-mindedly said, "Hello, Wade." He responded, "Hello, Steve."

Sisters Beth, Catherine, and Rebecca McKinney were all on our tennis team at one time. They made up half the team and were most successful.

The dad of a brother and sister at MA snored badly. They and their mother ordered a device that attached to the pillow case and was battery powered. When it arrived, they secretly attached it under his pillow. It was sound activated, so when the snoring began, it was to emit a mild current, which was not to awaken the individual but to cause the snoring to stop. Something went wrong, when during the night, the "mild" electric current set the dad's hair on fire!

The Perrymans' answering machine carried an interesting message. It was recorded by Dick and stated, "Hello, you have reached the Perrymans. If you wish to speak to Jey, she is having to finish up her chores. If you wish to speak to Dick, he is grounded for life, but if you wish to speak to Susan, the perfect child, leave your name and number."

There is another great picture of a Hero Day. I was playing the role of Barney Fife, bullet and all, and Susan was the adoring Thelma Lou.

Anne Lane Bird was the daughter of the Headmaster. Her dad blames or credits me with her pursuing a career in science.

Lucinda Cox, the eldest of three sisters, was the first female manager of the MA football team.

A long ago student, Wayne Simms, used to make long distance calls to *Russia*. Comrades!

Kenny Kirkpatrick was in too big a hurry and closed his locker on his little finger and cut off its tip. Mr. Dyess drove him to the emergency room, where they inquired about the missing tip. Mr. Dyess called back to the school and directed Mr. Segrest to Kenny's locker. He used his pass key to open the locker. He found the fingertip at the bottom of the locker, wrapped it in his handkerchief, and delivered it to the hospital, where it was successfully reattached.

On the day of a scheduled French test, the teacher was absent, so the test was postponed. Upon hearing this, Misti (what a great name) Brookhyser proclaimed, "Yes! There is a God!"

There was a time when several MA students would bail at the end of their ninth-grade year and transfer to Jefferson Davis, where the academics were easier. A number of them would return to MA for their senior year for the prestige of an MA diploma. The trustees then adopted a rule banning withdrawn students from returning to MA, unless the family had moved. I have long admired Kelton Jones. At the end of her ninth-grade year, all of her close friends left for the greener pastures of J.D., but Kelton chose to stay and stick with the more rigorous course of study.

Sondra Furlow was an outstanding student who has kept in touch. Whenever she is in town, she brings her baby around for Mrs. Pittman and me to see.

We had a female transfer student who was a basketball player. As a transfer, she was not eligible to play her first year, but she lit up the varsity in practice, and anticipation was high.

The following year, she was again outstanding in practice but did not play well in games. One night the mystery was solved. Her dad was late to a game, and she scored six points in the first two minutes. Once her father came, she reverted to her previous game forms. Parents, there is a message here.

We had a very good softball player who in one game hit a line drive so hard that the other team's shortstop did not have time to get her hands up before the ball hit her in the head. The ball then bounced off and sailed out into medium left field where it was caught for the out. Fortunately, the shortstop was not injured.

This same MA girl was playing in a summer league on a team that was coached by a guy who considered himself a softball genius. As a catcher, the young lady let a pitch get away from her that allowed a base runner to advance. The coach jerked her out in the middle of the inning. In this league, everyone batted regardless of whether they were in the lineup or not. The next time it was this girl's time to bat, the coach was coaching at third base. On a pitch, the girl turned and lined a hard line drive right at the coach. He went down and I promise, because I was there, the ball went between his head and his cap, which came off as he dropped. The girl got a standing ovation from the fans in the bleachers.

After lunch one day, Mrs. Grant walked into her classroom to find an eighth-grade girl crying uncontrollably. Mrs. Grant asked her what was wrong and whether there anything she could do. Between sobs, the girl managed to get out that she was devastated because her mother was only allowing her to spend $800 at J. Crew this *month*!

On another occasion, Mrs. Grant was driving to school behind an MA family. They were having a good time, waving their arms, tossing their heads, and moving their mouths. It was obvious that they were singing together. Mrs. Grant thought how beautiful it was that the family was singing. Maybe family values were not dead. Later at school when she asked the girl what she, her brother, and parent were singing, the answer came back, "Everybody Must Get Stoned." Well now, about that family values thing …

Before extra credit was banned, Diana and Molly Buss had averages over 100 in my class, and Molly tied with Carrie Tompkins with highest all-time averages for me: 105. That year I had three sets of twins in the class: the Busses, Jack and Sarah Crosby, and Colin and Ashleigh Crawford.

Speaking of Sarah, she was a remarkable athlete and in Middle School girls basketball was a tenacious defender. To say Sarah was a competitor would be a vast understatement. At one point, when she was bowling, she became frustrated. But she forgot she was using a bowling ball, and not a soccer ball, and gave the ball a vicious kick. Result: one broken foot and a very enraged father.

Two sisters that bear mentioning are Lillian and Wesley Wilson. Lillian was one of those who always did more than she was assigned to do. She was an extremely neat young lady, but, conversely, her locker still holds the record for being the messiest. Honestly, I think there were things growing in there. Lillian appeared in a Lifetime movie listed as "Preppy Girl." She was and is drop-dead gorgeous. Wesley, just as bright and attractive, is an accomplished equestrian, at one time ranking either first or second in the nation in her category. She had the misfortune of being kicked in the face by one of her horses, which was a potentially devastating occurrence. The doctor stated that if the blow had been in a slightly different place, it would have been fatal. Fortunately, she retains her beauty and her skill in riding.

The Bentleys, Kristin and Ashley, are another memorable pair of sisters. They were remarkable students and marvelous tennis players. Ashley actually graduated from BAMA on a full four-year tennis scholarship and set the record for the most matches won at BAMA in a career. But in her youth, she was playing in a tournament one summer and let her frustrations show. Her mom marched onto the court and informed Ashley that she was not a Smith, naming a girl who was known for acting up on the court, but that her name was Bentley, and she was expected to act like one. Mrs. Ialacci did the same once with her son, Brent. We need more parents like these.

Ashley, along with Kristin, came to my retirement reception. Ashley even left medical school at UAB to attend, driving down and then driving back up for duty.

Laura Andreades had to be the most consistent student I ever taught. Her average for each of the four grading periods was a 94. Her grade on the first semester exam was 94. Thus her average was obviously a 94. It almost reached the point where I was tempted not to grade her tests and just put 94 on them.

I remember Ally Rea fondly for a number of reasons, but I guess the main one is that whatever charity drive was going on, she always contributed and brought something.

Lizzie Hobbs was the quintessential Southern belle showing grace, beauty, character, and intelligence. Her dad, the judge, has a wicked sense of humor as evidenced by his alias, "Rev. Chett."

Johnston and Krisie Stakely are certainly among the most polite brother-sister teams I had the pleasure of teaching.

The four Browns always brought class and intelligence to my classroom. Well, really three. Harris was smart enough to go somewhere else to school in the seventh grade. Beverly was a very good athlete who took her talents to cheerleading where she has excelled. Happily for our volleyball program, Sara went that direction.

Caroline Franklin has to be the best and most loyal fan of MA girls athletics. For any team she is not on, she is there cheering for them.

Elizabeth, Forrest, and Madeleine Flemming had it all—intelligence, talent, looks, and sterling character. It was always a treat to watch Madeleine and her best friend, Ellie Knight, arm-in-arm, skipping down the breezeway into my classroom.

Emily Pierce is an excellent example of the phrase, "Still waters run deep."

Frances Freeman may be the most consistently good Middle School volley ball player I have ever been around.

Megan Thompson, an outstanding Middle School cheerleader, was in my advisee group my last year, and she frequently would spark our group with some of her routines.

After telling a blond joke, there is no telling how many times I came close to being pummeled by Lollie Garrett. Of course, I discovered that blond jokes really did not apply to Holly Harrold.

Every day, following an episode of the TV show *24* the previous night, Barton Crum and Elizabeth Kelly and I would hash it over. I always thought Jack Bauer would make an "interesting" Headmaster. If a teacher was not getting the job done, or if a student was misbehaving, Jack Bauer would just call them in his office and shoot them!

It took about six months of the school year, but I finally broke Dustin Weil of starting everything he had to say with "wait." It did not take as long to cure Maize Chambers of starting everything with "okay."

Sydney Anderson has it all—a wonderful student and a wonderful person to go along with her looks, which her grandfather would say she inherited all from him. Actually, her grandfather, Harry Anderson, is a hero of mine. He was my principal when I was at Goodwyn, and I have never known a better school man. He ran the school with an iron hand, and his philosophy was to weed out those who were interfering with serious students who were trying to learn. I could write a book about Harry.

Florence Ellen Young and Lucy Coleman were a dynamic duo in their days at MA. I recall telling Florence Ellen when she was in the seventh grade that she was "a teacher's dream," and that is the truth. Thanks to the notices that went out regarding my retirement, I have been able to reconnect with her.

The last of the terrific trios would be Haley Andreades, Grace Haynes, and Meredith Lee. I'll have more to say about them in the athletic section of this book. If extra credit had not been abolished midway through her seventh-grade year, Haley would seriously have challenged for highest all-time grade average. Her dad still has a note I sent home saying that her grade of 100 on a test brought her average down. I actually reached the point where I would use Haley's paper as the key to grade the others. Early in the year, I had checked an answer wrong on her paper and then discovered that she was right and I was wrong.

I taught a brother and sister who were as different as night and day. The guy would leave a test, smiling and proclaiming that he aced it. In truth, when he got the paper back, he earned a 57. The girl would go out wagging her head sorrowfully and then ace it with 97.

A new student, not knowing we notified parents when students failed a test, went home and told her mom that she had the highest grade in the class. The morning after the letter reached home, the mother came into my room dragging the wayward daughter by the ear.

Hendrick Adams and Erin Budney are on my gold list. In fact, if you ever saw the TV show *"The Golden Girl,"* then you will understand why the show could have been named after Hendrick. I had told the class about my favorite childhood candy, Charms, and bemoaned that it was not available any more. Hendrick and Erin went online and found a source for me, and now I am no longer Charmless. (Well, candy-wise anyway.) Erin is a fabulous soccer star, and she "ain't exactly chopped liver in cross country."

On another matter, Erin put things in perspective. We had had a preschool faculty meeting with a visiting speaker. He was one of "those" kinds of speakers who said that if you crossed your arms while you were being spoken to that meant you were rejecting what was being said and were "blocking" the other's words. So, one morning between classes, I stepped into Mrs. Grant's room and saw Erin standing there with her arms crossed. I asked Erin if she knew what having her arms crossed meant. She replied, "It means I'm cold." Leave it to a student to take the practical approach and put things into perspective. Perhaps, Erin should have been the speaker at our meeting.

Sara Walker became the very first student I taught to go through the entire year without missing a single daily quiz question.

Another winsome young lass was Skyla Parco. This was evidenced by a lad in seventh-grade science who spent more time staring at her than he did looking at me.

Walton Upchurch and Evelyn Smith were, and still are, best friends. I treasure two notes I received from them. They expressed appreciation for my having held their feet to the fire in science class. They expressed that they were given nothing and had to earn their grades by studying and hard work and that there were no "extras" given to guarantee passing grades, nor those of an A.

Andrea Gray Jones has come a l-o-o-o-o-ng way as a basketball player, because as a seventh grader, she would have three fouls on herself before the National Anthem was finished. One thing for sure: the gum she chews in a game is definitely going to Heaven, because …

In the lunchroom one day, Steve German watched a student walk by and remarked that the student was working on a third chin. Actually, in the Easter play, this young man could have played either the role of the multitude or the stone that was rolled away.

Drake McGowin is an elite gymnast, but we could never talk her into doing flips at halftime of our Middle School girls basketball games. Drake is also the reigning state pole vault champion.

When she was in my advisee group, Carolyn Parish proclaimed it the best advisee group ever! Who am I to disagree with Carolyn? All my advisee groups had one distinction. In all the years, we never even finished as high as third in the homecoming decoration contests.

When my son was a senior at Huntingdon, he house-sat for a mom and dad who were on a trip. Included in the deal was the junior high son. It happened at the time of an MA dance, and the parents had left money to cover those costs. Steve asked the boy if he had ordered a corsage for the girl he was taking. The boy replied that he thought he would just pocket the money and pick some flowers from the backyard. Steve immediately hauled him to the florist, remarking that the boy's date certainly had pretty eyes, but they were obviously not functional.

Our teachers and students are not just bright but talented as well. In addition to another student that I will mention later, I have paintings on my walls at home done by Ali Boozer, Jordan Hughes, and eighth-grade science teacher Jennifer Grant.

As a teacher, did I like some students better than others? Guilty. Did I not like some as well as others? Guilty, or maybe I did not like their attitudes or characteristics compared to others. I always told the kids at the first of the year that I would treat them just like they treated me. Did I actually dislike some students? I am afraid so, but I can truthfully say that I could use the fingers of one hand to count the kids that I just did not like. Also, I can honestly say that my feelings for every child I taught, positive or negative, did not affect their test grades at all. In fact, I never looked at a child's name when I graded a paper.

One year, a seventh-grade boy had written on his first test paper, "I have *screuded* up this test." That is the way he spelled it, and he had.

My first seventh-grade class is at least one of my most memorable. They won the Headmaster's Cup three consecutive years. Wanna bet that never happens again? I can still remember most of their names and had the privilege of teaching many of their children. During those days, on every Wednesday, we had fried chicken, rice and gravy, and rolls. There was a sweet young lady, Mikie Hammer, in the class whom the guys delighted in calling Hammerhead. Except on Wednesdays. You see, Mikie did not like fried chicken, so on Wednesdays she was Mikey, as in, "Mikey, may I please have your chicken?"

If I start naming names, I will inadvertently leave out someone important to me, but I must mention Jill Morrison Johnson. Jill flew in from Texas for my retirement reception. You think that doesn't mean something to me? Beth Weiss Wimbererly, class of 1993, gets second place for driving up from Florida, and as already mentioned, Ashley Bentley took off from medical school to attend, along with her sister, Kristin. Chapman Rice drove in from Tuscaloosa to attend. How can I say "thank you"?

That first class had more members at the reception than any other, and it was my pleasure to go out and eat with several of them afterward.

One year, we had a contest among the four seventh-grade science classes at night in the cafetorium. Each class chose three students to represent their group, and the contest was on the *Jeopardy!* format, so we called it "Sciepordy." The Bentleys' grandparents, Bo and Sweetie, drove from Sylacauga to see their granddaughter in action.

When Carol Brewbaker was going to get married, the lucky gentleman was not a southerner! He was from *Michigan*! Before allowing the marriage, Carol's brothers, Billy and Dick (a dyed-in-the-wool "suthenah," Suh), thoroughly indoctrinated him in the customs and culture of the *South*. I was very fortunate not only to get to teach Carol but also her three daughters, all quite bright and budding track stars.

Julia Steinhilber was a perfect example of beauty and brains. I believe it was when she was an eighth grader that she had all four wisdom teeth pulled at once. The procedure did not go well for her, and she was out of school for two or three days. When she returned, her face was still bruised, but she obviously has recovered from that condition. She was a very good athlete whom I had hoped would play basketball. However, she opted for cheerleader and was excellent.

Julia was a cheerleader when this incident happened before a football game. While our cheerleaders were warming up, the opposing school's band marched by them. One of the band members called to one of our cheerleaders, "You all must be rich." The cheerleader asked why he said that. He responded, "All of you have straight teeth." You parents who have paid for those $traight teeth can identify with the statement.

When she was a senior, Julia wrote an excellent article in the Upper School newspaper, *The Flyer*. It was entitled "The Pursuit of What?" It took a lot of courage for her article to include such phrases as, "The school must have been excellent at one time," and "The Montgomery Academy has kicked off its fiftieth anniversary with no excellence whatsoever. Let's do something about that." Whether you agree or not, it was a most thought-provoking article.

There were two other sisters, both quite bright, but they each spent more time at my desk on test days than they did at their own desks. Despite their best efforts, they could never get me to tell them the answers to any questions.

If you look up the word *class* in the dictionary, you will find the pictures of Lauren and Catie McRea. Lauren chose cheerleading over athletics, and when Catie came along, there was quite a tug-of-war for her contributions. She opted for athletics and won the Jimmy

Hitchcock Award. While I was assisting Julie Sinclair with coaching the girls JV basketball team, Catie came to us one day and said she was worried that she was taking too many shots. When have you ever heard that?

For a few years, we kept guinea pigs in my classroom, so three guys built a very nice split-level cage for them. There was Rusty, a male, and two females, Blondie and Bandit, who was a beautiful animal.

At some point, Bandit became heavy with child, so one day when I was teaching, I paused in mid-sentence. The students said my mouth dropped in wonder as I gazed at the cage. There was Bandit running along with three little balls of fur running behind her. The births had noiselessly taken place in five minutes.

At one time, I had the tenth-grade biology class keep a "baby," a boiled egg for a week. Everywhere they went, to church, ball games, dates, etc., the egg went with them, no egg-sitters. They also had to keep a journal detailing how much it would cost for clothes, food, diapers, and whatever else to take care of a baby for a week. It was in my fifth year that Allison Richbourg had a detailed baby book for "Eggbert." Thirty years later, upon my retirement, I mailed her the book, which her children have delighted in. We later switched to ten-pound bags of flour to make the baby experience more realistic.

We had another project while studying the nervous system. To gain an appreciation for the handicapped, students had to give up a sense or ability for one day. Ruth Penton Hayes lost her ability to speak. Her mom sent me a note asking if we could extend the project for a month. Ruth Penton has achieved her ambition and has become a successful dentist.

Two other students elected to be blind by wearing blindfolds. Ignoring the biblical admonition regarding the blind leading the blind, they attempted to help each other and wound up on the football field.

For most of my career at MA, after each test, I would put a chart on the board. The chart showed each class period, the number of As, Bs, and so on in each class, along with the average grade and the name and grade of the high scorer. In the last few years, due to "privacy" issues, I was not allowed to put the high scorer's name on the board. I wasn't putting the *low* scorer on the board, for goodness sakes. Thus, I really got a kick when an alumnus gave the graduation speech and mentioned that when he started seventh grade, his goal was to get his name on the board in my class and that motivated him to study hard and get good grades. Score one for "the good old days."

Well, guess what? it is *not* a violation of the Federal Privacy Act to put students' names and their grades on the board. This is ascertained by *Connelly v. Comptroller of Currency (*5th Cir. 1989), *Olberdling v. United States Dep't of Defense (8th Cir. 1983),* and *Lengerich v. Columbia College (*N.D. Ill. 2009). Thus, lawfully, I could put every student's grade on the board. However, I was only putting the highest grade on the board as a way of recognizing and commending hard-working, good students. So, this begs the question ...

A few records bear listing. The lowest grade on a test was a 1! That is right. Not a 0. We had fifty fill-in-the-blank questions at 2 points each. This particular girl missed 49, got one right, but misspelled it for half-credit, hence a 1.

Hollie Johnson and Steve Jones set the record for the most consecutive questions answered correctly on a series of grades, 108. Molly Buss and Carrie Tompkins had the highest yearly average: 105. Sarah Paige Massey had the highest grade on a final exam, 98.

This story that must be told, and I hope everyone will learn from it. At a football game, a student walked up to me and asked if I remembered her. She had been in my seventh-grade class a couple of years before and had transferred to another independent school that we were playing that night. We had a nice conversation, and then she asked me if I was still teaching about eating disorders. I replied that I was. She then asked if I was aware that she was anorexic while she was in seventh grade at MA. I really did not answer, but asked her if she knew what caused it. She said she certainly did.

She related that she had never been in the "in" crowd but badly wanted to be. In the summer before seventh grade, she got a telephone call from one of the members of the clique, inviting her to go to the movies at The Rave the next afternoon. She was thrilled and dressed appropriately. She had her mother drop her off early to be certain she would not be late.

After waiting for an hour and a half, the young lady called the house of the girl who had invited her. She said that when she asked where everyone was, the other girl replied, "You don't really think we would let you be a part of our group, do you? " and the girl said she heard other girls dying of laughter in the background.

This is an abominable act. Fortunately, the student had found a friend who had also had an eating disorder, and this friend had gotten her into a youth group at a church. At the time, she was doing well. However, just as with alcoholism, no one is ever cured of anorexia. I hope there is a lesson in this.

To close this section on a much happier note, there is a young lady—and she knows who she is—who made a bad mistake, a near-fatal one, but survived and has turned her life around and has become a very happy person, a role model, always with a huge smile on her face.

Also, MA students are involved in so many service activities such as Community Service Days, H.E.A.R.T., Interpersonal Relations, and many more.

I want to present two sterling role models for all MA students. A few years ago, the grade for an exemption was a 90. Charlie Hudgins had an 83 at the end of the first semester and asked me what he needed to be exempt from taking the final exam. I explained that it was mathematically possible, but I did not see it happening, as students' averages generally go down, rather than thirteen points up, during the second semester. Guess what? He made it!

The other feel-good story is Adele Walter. Most of her school life at MA, Adele was beset by one illness after another, which caused her to miss a lot of school time and to constantly struggle to catch up, much less keep up. When you are sick, you do not feel like studying, so naturally, your grades are going to suffer. Couple this with moving away for a year, then returning to MA—that's not a formula for success. The doctor finally decided to remove Adele's tonsils. She got healthy, and in both semesters of her senior year, she made straight As! Additionally, she is a talented artist, and I am in proud possession of two of her paintings. One hangs in my living room; the other is in my "memorabilia" room.

So Charlie and Adele, I thank both of you from the bottom of my heart for showing what perseverance and commitment can accomplish, and there is definitely a positive lesson for all students in this.

I want to dedicate this section to the students, past, present, and future, at The Montgomery Academy. You have kept me motivated and helped make my life so happy. God bless each of you.

5

PARENTS

Unreal, but true. I had to call the mother of a student who was disrupting the class. Her response was that the next time her darling misbehaved, I should walk over and slap the child sitting next to him. She said that would frighten her son so that he would not misbehave any more.

Audacious? That is an understatement, but it just indicates how delusional a very few parents can be when it comes to defending and rationalizing their children's behavior. I personally believe most of these few are unwilling to admit their own failures as parents. Instead, they want to shift the blame elsewhere. Unfortunately, you do not have to pass a test to become a parent, and there are no do-overs. As Wade Segrest so famously and accurately said, "The acorn does not fall too far from the tree."

In my experience at The Montgomery Academy, my relationships with parents have been 97 to 98 percent positive and supportive. Unfortunately, too often it is the other 2 to 3 percent high-maintenance parents that get the attention. A colleague stated that some people get a master's degree in "How to be Offended." Also, I have heard more than one teacher and coach remark that the percentage of teacher-parents who are hard to deal with regarding their child is higher than that of other parents. This was true in the classroom and in athletics—some in *both*!

It would seem to me that if any parent has had an issue with three or more teachers or coaches, then perhaps, just perhaps, the fault was not with the teachers and coaches. Perhaps that is time to take a realistic look at the child or in the mirror.

Hollie Johnson's dad, the late Tom Johnson, was the owner-publisher-editor of the *Montgomery Independent*. He was the finest newspaper writer I have ever read, with a wonderful way with words. I suspect the man is not turning, but rather spinning in his grave at the direction the paper has gone in since he sold it.

Hope Sorrell's dad had been a classmate in dental school with my brother-in-law, Bill. Hope's dad would frequently invite Bill over for a Coke because that is the only time his wife would let him have one.

Melinda Hornsby's grandfather, Leon Hornsby, was my science teacher in high school, so what goes around, comes around.

Eighth grade earth science teacher, Mrs. Grant, got a call one Sunday afternoon from a parent. The parent told Mrs. Grant that her son had gone hunting with his father and that she, the mother, needed the instructions for the project that was due the next day so that she could finish it for him.

It was well established that one parent wrote the term papers for her children, which certainly at least partially accounts for the difficulty they ran into in college.

Gretchen Lee's dad, Shon, once saved an Alabama victory over Auburn by knocking a loose ball out of bounds to prevent Auburn from recovering it.

Harold and Molly McLemore were the only father-daughter basketball players I coached. Harold was captain for me at Goodwyn, and Molly made an extremely brainy play at the end of a game with St. James.

A prominent businessman came to MA complaining that there was something wrong with the math curriculum because all of his children had failed math. Hm? This is the same man who, when the board was going to institute an alcohol policy several years ago, stood up and protested because he and his son drank together every night. A lady stood and said to him, "Sir, are you aware that you are breaking the law?"

One MA parent fancied himself a basketball coach. When the girls' varsity would play, he would sit in the front row and "coach" loudly the entire game. He never shut up!

Another MA baseball parent, whose son was a pitcher, showed how much he cared about the team. An error led to the opponents' scoring three runs. As the son walked off the field at the end of the inning, the father yelled, "That's okay, 'Jimmy,' this did not hurt your ERA."

As with MA parents, the parents of players on opposing Middle School girls basketball teams have been very nice. One notable exception was in a game when Lizzie Beale stole the ball and was headed for a layup. One parent of a player on the opposing team stated, "Put her in the wall!" (I have it on DVD.) What kind of example and teaching of your child is this? These are twelve- and thirteen-year-old girls, for crying out loud!

I have one last tale, and then a tribute to the 97 to 98 percent. The spring prior to my retirement the next year, at the end of class one day, a seventh-grade girl said, "I am *never* going back to a girls soccer match.

I asked, "Why not?"

She replied, "MA parents are an embarrassment. They think they are coaches. They run up and down the sidelines yelling instructions the whole match. They need to get them a team and coach it." This from a thirteen-year-old. Makes you wonder who is who.

Now to the approximately 5,000 parents who have been so kind and supportive during my thirty-five years, a huge, "Thank you so much!" That is a very poor way of offering my appreciation, but I have given thanks for you in my prayers. Your spirit of cooperation and many kindnesses have been awe-inspiring. Again, the old adage, "The acorn does not fall far from the tree."

I get into trouble when I start naming names because so many deserving parents get left off, but you know who you are because you have done so much. I am thinking particularly of the parents of my last few basketball teams. I must mention these parents: the Rices, who gave up a Super Bowl trip (more in the following section about this); (already mentioned) David Rees who gave me Casey Stengel's walking stick; the John Virdens who gave me the huge Daniel Moore painting of Gene Stallings's BAMA national championship; the William Haynes family who have kept me supplied with BAMA paraphernalia and reading material, as well as a close friendship; and Bob Ramsey who always provided me with a willing and helpful sounding board. Marty and Nancy Lee, as well as with Tommy and Jenny Andreades, have proven staunch friends.

To all of you, I thank the good Lord that he sent me your way and that you granted me the privilege to teach your children. I hope that my efforts have met your standards and have pleased you.

6

COACHES

A Montgomery Academy coach once remarked, "My ability as a coach varies from one game to the next, not depending upon whether we win or lose, but based upon how much playing time 'Lisa' got."

Coach David Bethea once sent his second string in on defense. On three consecutive plays up the middle, the opponent gained 12, 14, and 18 yards. Coach Bethea yelled, "Where in the world is Billy [the middle guard]?"

A voice from close to him asked, "You call me, Coach?" Billy (not his real name) had failed to enter the game, and we were playing with ten guys.

A dad had been complaining about his son's lack of playing time, so with time for one play in a scoreless first half, and the opponents on their own twenty-yard line, the coach put Junior (not his real name) in at cornerback. It happened. The other team's quarterback completed a long pass over Junior for an eighty-yard touchdown—the only score in a 6–0 game.

MA has had a fabulous athletic history, even more amazing considering it is a small, academically oriented school. There have been numerous state championships and very high all-sports yearly rankings statewide, covering all schools 1A to 6A. In 3A, MA has dominated state rankings in all combined sports.

Our tennis and golf teams have been fabulously successful, and MA claims at least one state championship in most sports. This in spite of the Alabama High School Athletic Association's ruling that all private schools have to count each student as 1.3 students, thus bumping MA up one classification. When our girls basketball team won the state tournament a few years ago, Dr. Johnson noted that all members of the team, save one, had been enrolled since kindergarten. So obviously, we had gone out and recruited four-year-olds knowing that they were going to be championship basketball players.

Since the school stresses academics, it is amazing how the student-athletes do it. They have to practice, then go home to spend hours on homework. Hopefully, they can find time for some social life to keep their lives balanced.

One student, who was an excellent athlete, transferred to MA because she was not being challenged in her studies at her former school. There was absolutely no contact with this student from any MA coaches. In fact, the coaches steadfastly avoided any contact with the young lady. An official at the other school was overheard commenting, "I do not understand why this would happen, unless it was for academics." Well, DUH, isn't that what school is supposed to be for?

There were four athletic directors (ADs) during my stay. Joe Mooty is a legend at MA. He coached football, won a state championship in baseball, but his legacy at MA was as boys varsity basketball coach. Joe was strictly old-school, a trait I greatly admire, and he adhered to the old-style virtues. He was a stickler for details and held his boys to high standards, both morally and in accountability to the team.

One of his former players told me that he had asked to miss practice once and that Coach Mooty told him to go ahead, but not to bother to come back. It didn't matter to Coach who it was, the rules were the same for all. The message was received. I still have a T-shirt from his retirement party that had a number of his maxims on the back.

Joe was known for being rather, er, "careful" with athletic department money. If a coach wanted to buy something, he or she had better have a very good reason.

Ann Boozer was hired to replace Coach Mooty when he retired. Dr. Johnson thought he was making history by hiring the first female AD in the state. It turned out that there was already a lady AD at another school. Ann did not lack for confidence in herself. She is the mother of Boomer and of "Ali Boo." Ali is an actress now, and one of her paintings hangs in my den.

The third AD, John Tatum, is another legend. John had been head football coach and an art teacher prior to accepting the position of AD. In addition to being a championship football coach, John was an excellent AD. I do not think anyone could outwork him. When an athletic event took place, he was *there*! He was accountable for his responsibilities and held coaches responsible for theirs.

Beneath an occasionally gruff exterior beat a heart of love. He developed a unique family atmosphere of love and respect among the members of his coaching staff. As Middle School girls basketball coach, I, maybe more than anyone else, appreciated John. He gave my sport the same support and just as much importance as he did any other sport.

If you valued your sanity, you never pulled a joke on John. You *knew* he would get you back, but it would drive you crazy wondering when. He might hold off for weeks, increasing your anxiety, until he got even.

I have two favorite funny memories of John. One was when he would get agitated. He would use the phrase, "I'll tell you one dad gummed thing!" The other—"Oh boy!"

In those days, on a Thursday night, the four Middle School and JV basketball teams would play Catholic. The two guys' teams would play at one school, and the two girls' teams at the other. On this night, the two girls' teams were to play at MA, and John was taking up money. A Catholic player in uniform came up and John said, "Son, the boys are playing at Catholic and it is girls who are playing here."

The youngster replied, "I *am* a girl!" John turned red as a tomato and apologized profusely.

John was planning to retire in a few years, but really left before he planned to and certainly before we wanted him to. He has spoken to several of us frankly as to the reason behind his premature departure, but it is his business whom he wishes to tell. Interestingly enough, he is now principal of the Upper School at St. James and is running a very desirable tight ship regarding discipline. He was a great loss to MA.

One of my saddest yet most gratifying moments at MA came on the last school day of John's career at MA. He came to my room to say goodbye and to wish me luck. On the way out, he told me, "You were one coach who never gave me any problems." Then with his characteristic honesty, he continued, "Yeah, you did, once." He paused, then continued, "But you were right."

Anthony McCall has the unenviable task of succeeding Coach Tatum, but he is doing well in a position in which the coaching staff has been hit with several unexpected departures. Anthony also has an assistant AD, Julie Sinclair, which previous ADs did not have.

I have seen numerous practices of various teams at MA and have observed many high-energy coaches with amazing work ethics. Unfortunately, I have also witnessed two or three who seemingly do not put much time and effort into planning and preparation and conducting of practice. I have always felt this was not fair to the players on their teams.

There have been so many outstanding coaches at MA that if I tried to list them all, I'd surely leave someone out, so I'll just name the ones that I was and am closest to.

I had the pleasure of being Ronnie (Knute) Elmore's basketball coach at Goodwyn. He was my captain and an awesome leader. I have never coached another guy who was as versatile as Knute. In his ninth-grade season, he led us to a State Junior High School Championship by averaging in double figures in scoring, collecting 321 rebounds, and, at 248 pounds, Ronnie would be the guy who would dribble out the clock when we were protecting a lead. There was no five-second rule then, and he never lost the ball.

It was one of my treats to serve on the MA coaching staff with him. He was an assistant football coach and varsity baseball coach. I even had him come in and work with my rebounders on occasion. Knute's baseball teams went to the state finals three of his last four years, but for some reason, that was not good enough. I know if my son played baseball, I would want him to play for Ronnie.

AD Anthony McCall has been an assistant football coach and is boys varsity basketball coach. His teams have been most successful, and Coach McCall always conducts himself in a gentlemanly manner on the sidelines. One thing that has impressed me so is that several times he has come into Middle School girls basketball practice to lend his expertise.

One particular example that stands out occurred during my last year of coaching. Grace Haynes, a terrific all-around player, had a minor flaw in her shooting form that was throwing her shots off, and I was unable to get it corrected. Coach McCall came in to observe. He watched a couple of minutes, spent about three minutes working with her, and she became an excellent post scorer, even though she was usually shorter than the girls she was going up against. She was outstanding in the clutch. In fact, in the CCC championship game, Grace twice hit go-ahead baskets in the last couple of minutes. There are not many varsity guys coaches who would take the time or have the interest to come in and work with seventh-grade and eighth-grade girls.

Tim Bethea is an outstanding coach and a wonderful family man. He was an assistant football coach and for several years enjoyed working with his brother, David, coaching the Middle School football team. He was also the coach of several MA state champion golf teams. Tim was a great asset to MA, and it was a shame to lose him to Trinity.

Greg Glenn and David Jones were both very good varsity boys basketball coaches, and both experienced successful tenures at MA.

In his short stay, Billy Beck was a definite plus to the school. Billy is a very conscientious individual. His departure was most unfortunate for the students at MA. We have lost entirely too many good men in the past few years from our athletic staff.

I only got to know Casey Smith, Chris Cournoyer, and Robb McGaughey during my last year, but all three are fine young men who are dedicated to their craft. Chris's golf team won the state championship in his first year as their coach.

A few years ago, Debra Cross assumed the responsibilities of softball coach. The second day of practice, the six seniors quit. When asked why, their response was that they did not realize they would have to practice and work and sweat. They just wanted to lie around and sun. Hmmmm, maybe they should have joined the "Worship the Sun God" team. Debra did a good job with the girls who wanted to play, and her daughter, Danielle, went on to earn a softball scholarship.

Denise Tinney has been girls varsity tennis coach for four years. The result? Three state championships, plus numerous all-state players. There are certainly more to come with most of her players quite young. Denise takes her position very seriously. She doesn't just show up at the match and make out a lineup, letting private coaches do all the coaching. She is a demanding practice coach who is on the courts with her girls whenever she can find the space.

Glenn Sylvest wears many hats at MA. In addition to teaching Lower School PE, he is an assistant football coach, girls soccer coach, and coaches so many girls basketball teams that I have lost count. Seriously, for the last few years, he has been a fine head coach of the girls varsity and girls Middle School teams, while assisting with the girls JV team. His teams are known for their suffocating presses with which they smother the opposition.

Glenn was my boss for the last few years when I was Middle School girls basketball coach, and although we did not agree on everything, he always supported me 100 percent, for which I am so appreciative.

If I had to be in a foxhole, Rick Cahalane would be the guy I would want to be in there with me covering my back. Look up the word *loyalty* in the dictionary, and you will see Rick's picture.

Rick came to MA as strength and conditioning coach and assistant football coach. He became an assistant track coach. His weight room work was great. He especially brought our girl athletes to a new level, and the results showed on the court. Rick then became our head football coach, and in his first year, his team beat Trinity, St. James, Alabama Christian, and Catholic, a monumental task.

Rick would literally go to the wall for a friend as he did for me on one occasion.

After he left MA, he had gone by the bank in Clanton to cash a check. He then went to Wendy's to grab a burger. When he paid for it, a guy who was sitting with two girls got up and approached Rick. The guy said that he noticed that Rick had some money and that he was unemployed and thought that Rick should share it with him.

Rick asked him, "What did you say?" The guy repeated his statement. Rick responded, "Listen, buddy, if you do not back off, in just five minutes, one of us is going to be in Heaven or Hell!"

The guy decided that he was dealing with the wrong person and took his "trade" elsewhere. Rick is a guy you want as a friend, and I am glad he is mine.

Julie Sinclair's volleyball teams had won 1,025 matches and three state championships at the conclusion of the 2009 season. She has all sorts of Coach-of-the-Year awards. Her teams are always superbly prepared. Obviously, Julie is also a champion at promoting her program, and it shows.

What a lot of people do not know is that Julie is also a very good basketball coach. She had two different successful tenures as MA varsity girls basketball coach, taking one team to the Final Four and very successfully coaching the JV girls basketball team for several years. Whenever she was called upon to fill in as softball coach, those teams also won, so I am describing a winner and a champion. She too is a loyal and trustworthy friend who has given me much support over the years.

Ginger Lowe coached volleyball at Troy State University for nineteen years and resigned because she was not being allowed to enforce her policy on alcohol. It would seem transitioning to Middle School volleyball would be difficult, but Ginger has made it seem easy, with her teams capturing the CCC championship her first three years and placing second last season. Ginger's practices are very precise, with a large part of the time spent on fundamentals and drills. She and I share the same belief that if players have not been taught and drilled in the right way to do things, that in scrimmaging, they are only reinforcing bad habits. Therefore, most of her practices are spent on exercises such as arm extension, hand position, leg and foot placement, and angles. Not as exciting, nor as easy to plan and carry out as scrimmaging, but with her methods, girls do the right things in games. Additionally, she is a caring individual who treats her teams like family.

She, too, is an excellent friend and one that I am proud to claim.

David Bethea, the coach. His record speaks for itself: eighteen Middle School CCC Championships, nine undefeated seasons, five in a row, nine varsity boys state tennis championships.

David is a stickler for hard work. His teams are excellently conditioned and prepared for any situation and conditions that occur in games or matches.

But it is David Bethea, the man, that I wish to talk about. He does not just talk the talk, but he walks the walk. He is a strong Christian. He conducts Bible study classes and leads the Fellowship of Christian Athletes at MA.

David is the kind of friend everyone wishes he or she could have. He is a strong family man.

When David first started at MA, he had two science class preps, taught PE, and coached football, while taking classes at night. Whew!

I knew David also at Eastern Hills Baptist Church where we were teammates on the church softball team. It soon developed that we shared a passion for the New York Yankees and the Crimson Tide, so our friendship evolved and grew through the years. In my last several years at MA, it was my pleasure to spend most of the morning break time with David "solving all sorts of problems," whether it be political, sports, or any situation at MA, or just talking about our teams or families. I really miss those times.

The story that exemplifies David Bethea occurred in June two years ago. It was a Friday afternoon at about two o'clock when I started feeling pain in the right side of my back. It grew progressively worse, and I knew what it must be because my dad had suffered kidney stones. The pain got so bad that I thought I was going to die. Then it got worse and I was afraid I was *not* going to die.

With typical male stubbornness, I would not give in to it, until at *midnight* I knew I could not take it anymore. Who did I call at midnight? David Bethea. He and Jenny rushed right over. I told them I thought I could tough it out until Monday. They have gotten a big kick out of that statement ever since. Jenny, a nurse, informed me that I was going to the emergency room. I wasn't about to argue. They carried me out, and even though they had plans for Saturday, they stayed with me until 4 a.m.

After that blasted thing was extracted the following week, David subsequently drove me to the doctor three times, went to the grocery store for me, and even spent a night at my house to be sure I was okay. That is a FRIEND! He later set up a surprise retirement dinner for me at my favorite dining place, The Ox Yoke. But he can no longer call me "old," as he used to enjoy doing. He is now a very proud grandfather.

On a previous visit to The Ox Yoke, David and I left from MA in our teaching togs. The waitress remarked that we were indeed the original *Odd Couple*. As she put it, one of you is not old and the other..., one of you is dressed for church and the other..., and one of you has lots of hair and the other....

I want to close this section by paying tribute to our three sets of cheerleaders and their sponsors. These girls work very hard and most of their practice times are in the hottest part of the year, in the hottest part of the days. They rarely get to practice in air conditioning, so I salute and thank them.

7

MIDDLE SCHOOL GIRLS BASKETBALL

It was Friday night, the night before the CCC (Capitol City Conference) tournament. At the conclusion of our last practice, I gave the girls my best pep talk. One of the girls raised her hand and asked if she could say something to the team. I replied, "Of course," thinking she was going to say something inspiring to the team.

Her statement was this, "I just want to explain to everyone why my hair looks the way that it does."

In my younger days, I probably would have sent her home to fix her hair while the rest of the team concentrated on being ready to play. But I just thanked her for telling us. The next day, she played an outstanding tournament.

A longtime official greeted me at the beginning of a season with, "Are you still around, Methuselah?"

Three Montgomery Academy coaches rescued me from the scrap heap of discarded coaches. The first was Julie Sinclair. Julie allowed me to become her assistant coach while she was coaching the JV girls basketball team. I knew some basketball, but I learned from Julie how to coach girls. They have to be coached differently from guys, in a lot of ways. For one thing, they want to be taught. They do not think they know it all. They are not interested in juking and jiving; they want to do things the right way.

The second rescuer was John Tatum, the athletic director. After two years of my helping Julie, John approached me on the breezeway one morning and asked if I would do him a favor. He wanted me to become the coach of the Middle School girls team. Before he could change his mind, I jumped at the chance. I continued to remain Julie's assistant with the JVs and for two years with the varsity when she took that team.

So I was spending four hours a day after school on the gym floor and loving every minute of it. David Bethea once asked me how could anyone as old as I (ouch!) do that. The truth is that I love teaching, and I was a teaching-type coach. I loved every minute of it, and the girls energized me. Thus began nine of the happiest years of my life.

The third coach who dug me out was Ginger Lowe. When I left basketball she asked me if I would sit on the bench with her during Middle School volleyball matches and keep stats and serve as a sounding board. I readily agreed, and it has been a joy to do what I could for Ginger. She and I are very much alike. Maybe that is why I think so much of her.

So to you three, I offer a resounding "thank you!"

I must pay tribute to several people. Please forgive me for inadvertently leaving anyone out who deserves recognition.

First to my number-one son, Steve, who was my loyal assistant for the entire nine years. Steve is a professor at Samford and lives in Vestavia, so this meant getting up every Saturday morning and driving down for the game and again on the occasions when we had a weeknight game. Steve was invaluable, as I learned on the few occasions that teaching duties prohibited his coming down. Monetarily, he was not well compensated. In fact, all he got out of it from a financial standpoint was lunch every now and then. Also thanks to Steve's wife, Julibeth, who juggled their schedules and obligations for Steve to do this. And for the times she could come down to cheer us on too.

David Bethea was undefeated as a scorekeeper for us, helping on numerous occasions. David also served as an assistant coach during the times that Steve could not make it, as well as being an ear for me during break each day and offering advice and opinions—but only when asked to do so.

I had two student assistants, Nancy Stewart and Chapman Rice. They did not continue their basketball careers on the varsity, but they provided immense help and guidance for our young ladies. Meagan

German also served well as an assistant when she could break free from her duties in the development office.

There were numerous managers, stats people, clock operators, scorekeepers, and announcers who were part of our program, whom we could not have done without. I want to especially mention some gentlemen who videotaped our games. It was so important to be able to watch and see things, good and bad, that needed to be noted. They were Dennis Bailey, John Virden, Terry Price, and Dr. Brad Katz.

To all of you, and to those of you that I overlooked, a huge "thank you!"

Also a number of dads offered to help me coach the team. I would have loved to have had them, and they could have greatly contributed, but I never did this because of the potential for problems. I did not want anyone in the bleachers to be able to say that the only reason "Lisa" is playing is because her dad helps Coach Jones. Something like that can spread like wildfire and ruin a team. Whenever a girl was on the floor, it was clear that she had earned that playing time, not because a debt was being paid.

There were the few inevitable disagreements with some parents. I'll just give two examples. Shortly after a close win over Trinity, a dad approached me and said, "Coach, we need to do something about the number of shots 'Lisa' is taking." Translated: "I want my daughter to get to shoot more." Having already looked at the stats, I was able to reply, "You are right. Lisa hit 38 percent of her shots today and the rest of the team hit 11 percent, so I am going to spend the weekend adjusting our offense so that Lisa will get more shots."

Another parent frequently offered advice after a game. One time after hearing his breakdown, I asked him what time his office opened Monday morning. He told me that he opened at eight o'clock. So I told him that I was going to take a day off on Monday and come down and advise him on how he could improve his services. As Gene Stallings once said, "If I listen to the folks in the bleachers very much, I will soon be sitting up there with them."

There was another "interesting" exchange I had with a parent, this one occurring after my retirement. I was attending a varsity girls basketball game, and one of my former players was playing well. Her parents were seated right in front of me, and I leaned forward and complimented their daughter's play. Her mother turned around and said to me, "Coach Fincher [her current coach] is the only coach she has ever had that has taught her anything." OUCH!!!

Believing that discretion is the better part of valor, I leaned back and did not continue the conversation.

Now, to put things in perspective, I always felt that we were a three-part team. The parts were the players, the parents, and the coaches. For the most part, that concept was understood and was quite successful. By far, at least 80 percent of the team and importance was all about the girls.

Memorable Seasons

Each team in a coach's career is special and creates its own personality and memories. Although each team is special in itself, it seems to be a coach's first and last teams that are the most special. Following is a summary of each of these nine special seasons.

My first team was special because they used every ounce of energy and skill that they possessed. The team consisted of only two eighth graders, Emilie Reid and Laura Dozier, and thirteen seventh graders. Emilie and Katie Sasser were elected captains. Emilie could have played on the JV team, but asked to stay down. Emilie was more than a captain, in that she was like a big sister to all the girls and a fabulous leader. Statistically, she led the team in almost every category, including blocked shots. When Emilie blocked a shot, she put it in the bleachers. Her mom scolded her about that, saying that it wasn't ladylike. Thank goodness, this was one time she did not take Mom's advice.

This group was the worst shooting team I ever coached—shooting only 21 percent for the season. They won on a ferociously aggressive defense, rebounding, courage, and tenacity. Your life was in danger if you got between them and a loose ball, as I found out in practice several times. The team's picture at the end of the season reflected their dedication. The legs of Coleman Upchurch and Meagan Vucovich were green, purple, black, and blue from the number of times they hurtled to the floor to get a loose or bouncing ball.

Their courage was shown in that,despite being behind at the half during the last seven games of the regular season, they came back to win. In the semifinals of the CCC tournament, the girls rallied from a 7-point deficit in the first quarter to tie the game at the half. When I walked into the locker room, they yelled in unison, "WE'RE NOT BEHIND!"

Cameron Wolf was our point guard. She may have been tiny, but she was our engineer. Katie Sasser was difficult to shoot over and improved steadily as a rebounder, garnering 15 rebounds in the championship game.

Taylor (T-Bone) Ramsey could play point or wing, and in the last three minutes of a close game (weren't they all?), she would take over. She wanted the ball and would get it any way she could, via steals, interceptions, rebounding—whatever it took. In the clutch, her eyes had the look of an assassin's. She made one of the most incredible plays I have ever seen in the finals of the CCC tourney. She took a shot from the right corner, which missed and rebounded on the opposite side. Taylor got the rebound, meaning after she shot, she sprinted the baseline through the other players and got the ball. That describes the effort that won for us.

The first game keyed our season. We trailed at the half (what else is new?), but held St. Jude scoreless in the second half. Emilie Reid scored 21 of our 28 points, which would turn out to be one of only two times a player topped 20 points for us in a game during my nine years. Several could have done it several times, but we refused to have a "star" system because I was afraid if all your eggs were in one basket and that egg got broken, you were in trouble. This was borne out more than once in the future.

Perhaps our most exciting game of the year was against ACA. We trailed all three quarters, then with about twelve seconds left, Emilie somehow got an offensive rebound, put it back in, was fouled, and completed the old-fashioned 3-point play. Then, it seemed as if we had ten on defense, rather than the usual five. ACA finally missed a hope shot, and Coleman grabbed the rebound to end it. It was a typical game for us as seven of our girls scored against only four for ACA.

We only lost two regular season games, both to Hayneville ("those women," as Emilie called them), and went undefeated in CCC play.

In the CCC tournament the Lady Eagles only allowed Catholic 2 points in the second half, none in the final quarter, to win 19–11.

In the finals, in a change of pace, MA led from the get-go, beating St. James decisively, 23–11. Coleman was all-tournament, and Taylor was tournament MVP. The girls finished 12–2 and voted Emilie as the season's MVP.

I doubt there are many coaches out there who have heard this. We had done all I had scheduled for practice one night and finished about ten minutes early. When I told the team they were getting out early, they shouted, "No! Let us do another drill!"

To show you how aggressive our 1–3–1 zone defense was, Coach McCall complimented me on what a great man-to-man defense we had.

Coaching Middle School girls basketball (MSGBB) is a challenge in that you basically have to start with a new team each year. All eighth graders and the best seventh graders move up to the next level.

Ginny Gross and Meagan Vucovich were elected co-captains for our second season. Our motto, "We Believe," was coined by Lauren James. We also had a cheer in our before-the-tip huddle, "GIT 'EM!" expressing our defensive philosophy. At the end of each game, save one, the yell would be, "GOT 'EM"

Lauren perfected her signature move of coming from behind a dribbler and swiping the ball from her.

The season was marked by going to Hayneville and registering the first-ever MSGBB victory over "those women" by a score of 29–20. Meagan was out sick, and Sarah Crosby got her first start and scored 9 points. Their coach told me that he wished he could get his girls to play that hard.

I think we were still relishing our victory in the next game when St. James ended our seventeen-game CCC winning streak. It was our only loss of the season and our only regular season CCC loss in a three-year period.

Elizabeth Richards had a great move in which she would jump into our defender and shoot, and we would get called for the foul. It was similar to today's officials who let a low-post player back all over a defender and not be called for an offensive foul. Elizabeth made eight of ten free throws in the second half. After the game, I was going to their locker room to congratulate them, but was stopped by a couple of MA parents and warned not to do so because of a derisive and insulting chant they were chanting. We determined that if we could get them in the CCC tournament, they would pay. We did, however, win our second successive CCC regular-season championship.

In the CCC tournament, we defeated ACA 25–18 in the semis, and then came our longed-for chance at STJ. In a classic defensive match-up, the Lady Eagles prevailed 18–14, holding them to 8 percent shooting effectiveness! This was one of a very few games that I felt the officials (one in particular, "Porky") were biased against us. We shot six foul shots; St. James twenty-seven! Two STJ dads and their athletic director remarked to me after the game that the officials did their best to give the game to STJ.

Kate Lamar made a huge shot for us at the end of the game, and this was termed The Shot of the Year.

In the second half, Sarah took Elizabeth Richards man-to-man and held her to one field goal. Ginny Gross was selected all-tournament, and Claudia Cauthen was named the tournament MVP.

The team voted Ginny as the season's MVP.

One regret I have regarding season three is that there are no videos of this team. This was a high-scoring, run-and-gun type of team that averaged 42 points a game, playing six-minute quarters. They completed a third consecutive regular season title and were undefeated until the CCC championship game, which we lost by 2 points. The Lady Eagles outscored their opponents by an average of 25 points per game. Our planned fifth starter, Sarah Crosby, moved up to the JV team. Tri-captains Diana and Molly Buss and Nancy Stewart, along with seventh-grader Brittany Tucker, were the other four. The fifth spot was occupied by four other rotating players.

The Buss twins scored 216 points as Molly became our first player to average in double figures. Britt scored 106 points and led the team in rebounding and blocked shots.

Each season, I would give the girls a basketball handbook of tips, axioms, and other advice. Allison Tinney was the best at digesting all that material. Any sentence I started that came from that handbook she could finish word-for-word.

Our first game with St. James, fourth game overall, produced yet another interesting development. Following a 39–9 thrashing in their gym, the STJ girls left the floor without the traditional post-game handshake. A furious Lisa Bridgeman, the varsity girls coach at St. James, and the best varsity girls coach I have seen in my years, stormed to the locker room and ordered them back to the floor to shake hands.

We would have been better off not shaking hands at Hayneville following our 45–23 win. The Hayneville "ladies" pretended (I hope) to blow their noses on their hands prior to shaking hands. Sometimes you wonder where parents and coaches are.

Our biggest margin of victory was 63–9 over Trinity. No starter played in the second half, and thirteen of the fourteen players on the team scored.

In the CCC semis, we beat St. Jude 44–17, our thirteenth consecutive win that season. However, we encountered another episode of bad sportsmanship and poor leadership by a coach. In the second half, Huntley Chapman was bringing the ball up the court on a 3-on-2 fast break. She came to a jump stop on the foul line as she was supposed to do. A St. Jude player ran up behind her and deliberately pushed her hard in the back, causing an injury. The girl committing the foul laughed, as did her teammates and *coach*! What is being taught here?

It was after this game that I told John Tatum that I would never take another team to play at St. Jude because we got roughed up every time. I told him I would take a forfeit before I would go back there. He told me that we did not have to play them. Regardless of what anyone says, there is no regulation requiring any CCC team to play any other CCC team. Scheduling was done for getting more games played. I'll take fewer games for my players' health.

The finals resulted in a very disappointing loss to ACA, 28–26, as one of their girls hit a layup with five seconds left. Not meaning to take anything away from ACA, who had a fine team and a great coach, but I am convinced that if I had stayed home that day and not "coached," we would have won. One thing that will always stand out to me was Nancy Stewart's talk to the team after the game. It was all praise and encouragement and still sends chills down my spine when I remember it.

We were greatly blessed with a special guest at the tournament. One of the best female athletes in the history of the state, Courtney Carpenter, came down from Moulton to cheer for us. Courtney is in a wheelchair, paralyzed from the chest down following a tragic accident. Her presence meant more than words could ever express.

I also wish to pay tribute to Art Parker, a marvelous sports reporter and the best friend Middle School and Junior Varsity sports ever had. His attention has been sorely missed.

Nancy later told me that she slept in her uniform that night because she knew she would never get to wear it again. The loss began a two-year slide by the MSGBB teams as we failed to advance beyond the semifinals the next two years. Molly Buss was named to the all-tournament team. The squad also selected Molly as the team's MVP for the season.

It was told to me after the game that two of the seventh graders on the team, or their parents, or both, stated that unless they moved up to the JVs next year, they would play "Y" ball rather than play for me again. Obviously, this was over playing time, and that was certainly their prerogative. Never believe there is not drama in MSGBB. More than countering that, immediately after the game, Lanier (Lani) Smith and her mom approached me and told me that they wanted Lani back on the Middle School team next season. I was ecstatic, as I knew had my leader.

The next year was the year of the ScrapEagles. ACA and Catholic seemed to be a lot better than the other teams in the CCC, and, indeed, they did meet in the CCC finals. However, I am convinced we were only one player away from being a very good team.

Lani was our captain and a magnificent leader. In a home game versus TPS, we were playing badly and led by only 1 point at halftime. I would always give the girls a couple of minutes alone before I went to the dressing room. When I walked in, one of the girls said, "Coach, you don't have to chew us out, Lani has already done that."

Actually, I never considered myself as a chewing-out type of coach, and rarely a fussing one. I like to think I was a teaching coach who could instill pride in performance in the girls. But in preseason practice, Lani suffered a broken foot and missed the first three games. When she walked in wearing that boot, I don't know who was more devastated, Lani or me.

Beth Brantley did a very good job of filling in during that time. Beth was the ultimate effort player. I think there are still dents in the wall of the gym where Beth ran headfirst pursuing loose balls in *practice*! Katrina Dean led the team in blocks, rebounds, and scoring, hitting 60 percent of her shots. Hagan Froemming showed a unique ability in our 1–3–1 defense. At times, she was able to cover both the middle and point, thus freeing up our defensive point to concentrate on one player.

The ScrapEagles got off to a blazing 9–0 start; then we went to Catholic and met referee Thomas Jackson. Midway in the first quarter in which our defense had them in control and rattled, the Catholic coach called timeout and had a consultation with Mr. Jackson. Thereafter, surely a coincidence, Mr. Jackson informed me that we could not talk on defense, because it was "distracting." He and I had a discussion in which I demanded that he show me the rule in the rule book. He said he would show me at the half, but now we were going to play, and he blew his whistle.

Of course, when the buzzer signaled the end of the first half, he took off for the officials' dressing room. He came out right before the beginning of the third quarter. I immediately called timeout and confronted him. Julie Sinclair, who was JV coach at the time, joined the conference. After not being able to find any such rule, Mr. Jackson declared the ball in play.

Then in the fourth quarter, he said we could not wave our arms on defense as this was distracting. If it would not have gotten MA in trouble with the Alabama High School Athletic Association, I would have pulled our team off the floor and gone home. I do not think it cost us the game, because they were better than we were, but it did cost our girls a fair chance. We then lost the final two games of the regular season. In the semifinals, the girls came from way behind, making a valiant effort, to close within 2 of ACA, but went down to defeat. Lani was named all-tournament.

Lani and Katrina shared MVP honors. Mille Virden brought a special brand of toughness to the team, and special kudos go to Anna Harris. Anna, a true post player, wound up being our point guard on offense.

While a 7–5 record in the fifth season might be considered a good season in some places, it was not for us. I say this, not because of the record, but because we were not as good as we could or should have been in season number five. There was a chemistry problem on the team, which I could never solve. I do not know whether to classify it as bad chemistry or no chemistry, but I know exactly when the problem began, and it resulted in three definite cliques on the team. I consulted a number of people about how to deal with it, but no one had any answers. There simply wasn't one. It is a shame because, basically, they were all good kids.

Katherine Stewart, following in her sister's footsteps, and Sarah Donnell were captains, and they served well.

Mary Blan Frazer came on like gangbusters to lead the team in rebounds, deflections, and floor burns—a new category to keep up with how many times a player went on the floor to fight for a loose ball. Hagan led in scoring and set a record for blocked shots. Mille and Anna, who again played point for us, led in assists and steals, respectively.

A low light of the year came when Blaine Wise was bitten by a player whose dad became a prominent politician.

The team was called the Attackagles, and this tenacity was demonstrated when Mille jerked the ball out of the hands of a St. James player and put the ball in the basket in the fourth quarter of a very close game.

At Tallassee, Mary Blan hit two free throws in the last ten seconds in a 23–22 victory.

Things really bottomed out in every way when ACA led us 19–2 at the half. We made a great comeback, fueled by Katherine Bryan's three pointers, to lose by only 2.

As if things had not been bad enough, in the CCC tournament, we had only three healthy girls. Mary Blan was coughing every breath. Dr. Froemming told me that Hagan had taken seven pills that morning, and in the first three minutes of the third quarter, Mille went down with a badly sprained ankle. We still went toe-to-toe with ACA, losing by 2 in overtime. Hagan made the all-tournament team, and the team voted Mary Blan as the season's MVP.

I guess a microcosm of the season was explained in one game when I put in a sub, and she started playing awesome defense on an opposing player. The problem was, we had the ball!

Year number six began a fantastic run in which the girls would go 51–4 (51–3 after a season-opening loss to Prattville), 38–2 against CCC teams, and four consecutive CCC championships. I'm just glad they let me go along with them for the ride.

It began one day in the spring at the conclusion of a science class. Emily Bailey approached my desk and told me that she wanted to play basketball the following season. This was wonderful news. Emily had not played in the seventh grade. Her "Y" coach of her Lower School days had told me that she was the best player in the grade. Despite having sat out a year of experience, Emily became at least *one* of the most valuable players on the team by season's end.

The team was tabbed the SassAgles by Glenn Poundstone's mom who said that they were "short and sassy."

Summer workouts reached a new high as Lesley Shinbaum put in over eighty workouts and Malone Walker seventy or more.

Chapman Rice and Lindsay Doctson were elected co-captains. Chapman produced one of the most awesome examples of leadership, loyalty, and commitment that I have ever heard of. Her family was friends with Coach Richard Williamson of the Carolina Panthers. He called and offered Rush, Marti, and Chapman a full Super Bowl XXXVIII package that included transportation there and back, three nights at the hotel, and Super Bowl tickets.

Chapman immediately stated she was not going because we had games that weekend, and her place was with her team. Rush and Marti then declined to go and stayed and supported Chapman and the team. Wow! This is what you call loving your teammates and putting them ahead of yourself. I am sure that Coach Williamson, having played for Coach Bryant, understood and appreciated this. Chapman will obviously always occupy a special place in my heart.

Laura Bownes also had an example of commitment and loyalty. She had the opportunity to attend an invitation-only opening of a plush new restaurant in Birmingham, but she also declined, in order to be with her team.

Chapman was the only guard in my nine years to lead the team in blocked shots. Lindsay led in scoring and rebounding; Glenn led in steals; and Laura Andreades in assists.

If you had told me at any time that we would score 33 points in a game and lose, I'd have sent for the guys in the white coats with butterfly nets. But that is what happened in our first game at Prattville. The Lady Lions scored 36. We came back home and rededicated ourselves to two maxims that would be our theme the next four years: (1) "The day following a game, because you have defended her so closely, when an opposing player looks in the mirror, she will not see her face but yours," and (2) "We will defend our goal until the 'hot place' freezes over, then we will defend it on the ice."

Our other loss that year was at Tallassee, where we had our usual bad injury. I'll cover this in the next season discussion. Suffice it to say that when we played them at home, at one point in the game, Chapman was dribbling the ball up the court talking ninety-to-nothing to her defender. We all almost fell off the bench laughing. You'd have to know Chapman to appreciate this, as she was the epitome of the well-mannered Southern lady. When I asked Chapman what she was saying, she replied, "I told her that if she put her hands on me again, I was going to knock her head off!"

I never advocated, nor even approved of, rough play, but I had to admire Glenn Poundstone at Tallassee that season. We were taking our usual physical mauling there when Glenn went into the game. She immediately threw the prettiest cross-body block you have ever seen into one of their players, sending her into the bleachers. Next day, a number of football coaches were lined up at Glenn's locker trying to get her to play football the next year.

At Trinity, in a 20–15 win, Lindsay had sixteen of our points; Emily made a key rundown from behind, preventing a layup by swiping the ball from the girl's dribble; and Laura hit a key basket in the last minute.

An interesting episode occurred when we played Catholic. A few days following the game, I got a very nice letter from the Catholic coach telling me that some of his players told him that one of our players had been using very "unladylike" language on the floor. He felt I'd want to know about it. Middle School Director Jerry Brewer and I investigated but found no substance to the accusation. However, in talking to our team about it, one of our girls, a Catholic herself, said that, on the contrary, a few of the Catholic players needed to go to confession that week. As I said, MSGBB is never dull.

In the CCC tourney, the two best teams played in the semis when we beat Catholic, 28–20. After trailing midway through the second quarter, Chapman, playing her best all-around game of the year, hit a clutch basket, and Lindsay scored 14 points.

In the finals, the SassAgles blew Trinity away, 33–6, with eight different girls scoring. We held TPS to only one point in the second half and one field goal during the entire game. Emily Bailey dominated the boards and scored 7 points. "E-Bay" was named all-tournament and Lindsay, MVP of the tournament. Lesley Shinbaum, playing point guard, had only one turnover for the entire tournament. The team selected Lindsay as MVP for the season.

One of those unforgettable moments occurred during this season. Laura was an excellent shooter, but she was a seventh grader and tiny, so she had a difficult time getting untracked. It was in the third game that she scored her first basket. When she came to the bench, she exclaimed, "FINALLY!!!"

Year number seven got off to a unforgettable beginning in the spring. Mary Hendon DeBray came into my office and told me that she was not going to play next year. My world was crumbling when she yelled, "April Fool!" I had been taken bigtime. I vowed to get even, but I haven't yet. All Mary Hendon did the following season was be elected co-captain, along with Lizzie Beale, lead the team in rebounding and scoring, be named to the ALL-CCC tournament team, and be voted MVP for the year by her teammates.

The team was dubbed the RopeAgles from the old axiom, "Hold the Rope." Our "rope" (and we had an actual rope) was thought of as being made from five interwoven strands, each beginning with the letter L, which stood for loyalty, love, lionhearted, linked, and leadership. The team lost two games during the season, both to Trinity. They were disastrous as we scored 12 points in one game and only 7 in the other. I still have the actual rope that we carried to all the games. It sits on top of the team warm-up ball for that year.

The Shinbaum family was heavily involved. Lesley was our starting point guard. Scottie, her brother, kept stats; her father, Richard, was scorekeeper and announcer; and her mom, Nancy, threw her shoulder out of joint swinging the rope during the championship game.

This was the first year of an amazing three-year run in which we had incredible depth at point guard. This year, we could interchange Lesley, Lizzie, and Morgan Ramsey with no drop-off. In fact, there were times all three were in the game at the same time. Try pressing that group!

We were not fortunate injury-wise as Maggie Mardre, who was shooting lights out, suffered a bad ankle injury. Leslie broke her little finger, and Mary Hendon got a concussion at Tallassee. This was the third consecutive year a player had been hurt at Tallassee. Two years ago, one of our girls got a bad bite on her *head*! The previous year, Hannah Smith had her arm broken, and this time, the concussion. I am certainly not saying these were deliberate, but we elected not to play them again. I think a couple of our parents would have strung me up if I had.

Another incident occurred at home against them. I have never seen a coach exhibit such poor sportsmanship and be such a poor example as their coach was on this occasion. She got one tech, and the official told me that the only reason she did not get another was that their team had no other adult with them. It was so bad that two *Tallassee* residents wrote their superintendent about her. To their credit, she was not their coach the following year. We would not schedule them again after that third straight year suffering a bad injury against them. Actually, I'd rather play the Juilliard School of Music Fighting Harpsichords, or the Third-Grade Blind Little Sisters of the Poor.

Our "freeze the ball" game consisted of the three guards out front running the weave, while the other two would stand on the sideline on the left side of the court, thus opening up the middle any time one of our guards wanted to drive. I always got a kick out of Mary Hendon in practice when we did this, as she was one of the "standers." She was bored to death and would stand in her spot and twirl, dance, or do cheerleader routines.

On Friday night prior to the CCC tournament, yours truly went home, again afraid I was going to die, then becoming afraid I was not going to die. I felt even worse on Saturday, so Glenn Sylvest and Steve coached the team to a second successive CCC championship. There are two theories here. The first that I faked illness so that the team would win it for their dying coach. I'm not that smart. The second is that the thought of playing TPS again scared me half to death. Again, not true. I was anxious for another shot at them. I was just plain "nigh unto death," or at least quite sick.

In the semis, the RopeAgles coasted to a 21–6 win over Catholic. Between games, Dr. Froemming and Dr. Smith came to check on me. They gave a very plausible explanation for the reason for "home cooking" at out-of-town games. The officials are local. When they go to the post office or the grocery store or to church, it is not our parents they are going to see, but the local parents. They may even be employed by parents of some players on the local team. I am not implying that deliberate miscalls are made, but subconsciously, they may see things in a different light.

This does remind me of a story. Seems the devil contacted St. Peter and challenged him to a game between Heaven and Hell. St. Peter told him that was absurd, that all the great coaches were in Heaven. Satan replied, "Yeah, but all the referees are in Hell."

The finals brought one of those classic games that I am sorry I missed but am overjoyed that John Virden videotaped it for me.

Midway through the second quarter, we were behind, 10–0 to Trinity. Then Maggie Mardre hit a huge shot that seemed to ignite both our team and the fans. In a preview of something to come, Morgan hit a buzzer beater to close the score to 12–10 at the half. The RopeAgles shut Trinity out in the third quarter, taking a 16–12 lead. Malone made two big left-handed hook shots that some people might have thought of as luck for an eighth grader. It was not luck. It was because she probably practiced that shot over a thousand times in the summer.

The final quarter was a back-and-forth affair, ending in a tie. In overtime, Lizzie and A.T. hit quick baskets, but Trinity battled back. With six seconds left, Morgan hit a twelve-footer, then stole the in-bound pass to seal the victory. It was the Wildcats' only loss to a CCC team that season. Eight different MA girls scored. Mary Hendon was selected all-tournament, and Lizzie was the tournament's MVP.

Sarah Reid led the team in field goal percentage, and Adele Walter hit 100 percent of her free throws. A.T. Froemming blocked twenty-eight shots, but she was just warming up, and Lesley and Mary Hendon each had thirty-three floor burns.

The team voted Mary Hendon as the season's MVP.

In season number eight, MA went 13–1, going undefeated in CCC play starting a 27–1 run over the next two seasons. A.T. named the team the UnStopagles. In the summer prior to the season, Morgan had three progressive surgeries on the bottom of her foot.

Did that stop her? No way! Each afternoon the day of the surgery, she insisted on practicing, coming to the gym with one shoe and a bloody bandage and sock on the damaged foot. No one doubted her commitment and courage.

A.T. had an incredible seventy-two blocked shots for the season, averaging five per game. They were not all in the paint either. She would go out on the wings and the point to block or alter shots, or just simply to discourage any would-be shooter.

Laura Helen Swann led the team in rebounding. Four different girls, showcasing a balanced attack, scored over 50 points, with A.T. having the highest number. Morgan had fifty-one assists, and Haley Andreades led in floor burns and steals. Adele Walter, still playing through an unbelievable run of injuries and illnesses, displayed a deadly left-handed outside shot to have a 45 percent field goal percentage to lead the team. Adele was also the best right-handed dribbler for a left-handed person I know of. Lefties typically do not use their right hands very well. I have often wondered just how terrific Adele would have been if she could have had good health and luck. Margaret Virden was Miss Versatility. In one game, she played all five defensive spots and four of five on offense. Over the course of the season, she played all five on offense too. Co-captains were Sydney Anderson and Sarah Reid Harris. The team scored 420 points and gave up 185.

Our defense carried us the first four games, highlighted by a 2-point win over TPS, in which Margaret scored the tying basket. Then on an out-of-bounds play, Laura Helen actually picked two Wildcats, Haley made a beautiful pass, and Margaret scored the winning goal. To finish the day, she rebounded the ensuing Trinity miss and dribbled out the clock. It was in this game that I had severe chest pains, but decided if I was going to die, what better place than at the gym with my team.

Following the game, Coach Tatum insisted that I go to the emergency room. I told him that I was going home and would call the doctor on Monday. About thirty minutes after I reached home, my telephone rang. It was my primary care physician, Dr. Hendon. John Tatum had called him. Dr. Hendon instructed me to go to the emergency room *right then*. I had five stents implanted. So you can blame Coach Tatum for my still being around.

The next week, we had practice scheduled, and as Ginger Virden was driving Margaret and Haley there, she asked, "Do you think Coach Jones will be there?"

Margaret replied, "Oh, if he can walk, he will be there."

I love having that reputation! At Wetumpka, Sydney scored the decisive basket in the final minute, and then while we were freezing the ball, a big Wetumpka girl jumped on Haley's back, and Haley was called for *traveling*! In the third game at STJ, Laura Helen had thirteen rebounds.

We were quite honored in our game at Catholic. Coach Cliff Ellis, who had just left as coach at Auburn University, came to the game. He was a close friend of Sarah Reid and her family. After the game, he came into our locker room and spoke to the girls and complimented them on their play. We all deeply appreciated that.

The second game with Trinity was another classic matchup. Trinity led the entire game. With just under a minute to play, Haley hit an eighteen-footer. She then sealed the deal with a break-away layup for a 4-point win. We played poorly and lost at Prattville, but that might have served as a wake-up call, as that was the team's last loss in the next year and a half. In our return match with them, we blistered them 35–16, with Sarah Reid leading the way with 8 points.

In the semis, nine Unstopagles scored as MA led Catholic 17–2 at the half on the way to victory.

The third meeting of the year with Trinity for the championship was a dandy. Trailing 8–5 in the first quarter, MA held the Wildcats scoreless for the next two and one-half quarters, winning 38–13, despite the Wildcats' shooting seventeen free throws to MA's one. (That was justified, as we really got after them.) Trinity scored only three field goals the entire game.

Sydney Anderson, "The Long Ranger," hit three 3-pointers in the game, giving her four for the tournament (both MAMSGBB records), and she was named the tournament's MVP. Her granddad may still be on the street corner holding up her award. Laura Helen had ten rebounds, and Haley, making herself an absolute defensive pest, had 8 points, six steals, and two deflections, along with three floor burns. Laura Helen joined Sydney on the all-tournament team.

At the end-of-season banquet, Morgan, A.T., and Margaret shared the Player-of-the-Year Award. Meredith Lee and Grace Haynes shared the Steel Magnolias Award for their robust aggressiveness. 'Twas said that before they would pair off against each other in practice that they would shake hands and apologize to each other in advance for the lumps they were about to raise on each other's noggins.

Finally, John and Ginger Virden and Dr. Mark and Benita Froemming were given the "Bear for Punishment Award" for having put up with me for four years, as each of their two daughters played two years on the Middle School team, meaning each of the parents served four years.

In colleges and large high schools, it is possible to use the same system each year because you can get the players you want to fit into it. However, in small high schools, you do not have that luxury, so it would seem prudent to adjust the system to the abilities of the personnel if you wish to maximize the skills and the potential of the team.

We rarely ran the same offense in two consecutive years, but in the 2006–2007 season, if ever a system and the players were meant for each other, this was it—the perfect marriage.

Haley Andreades, our point guard, was an awesome passer who could see the floor amazingly well. It did not hurt that she shot 45 percent to lead the team either. She led the team in assists and floor burns. She was quick as a hiccup and was a terror on defense, setting a season's record for steals. Like the other four starters, Haley was an honor roll student.

Erin Katz, another excellent passer, played wing on offense and defense. She was Haley's back-up at point also. She made some unbelievable no-look passes during the season. On defense, she was fast, tough, and had a little, er, meanness in her on the floor. Actually, all these girls were extremely aggressive on the floor and wonderful young ladies off the court. I never heard a single complaint from any teacher about any of them, academically or conduct-wise. In previous years, we would try to influence an opponent's offense to their left, but not this year. We wanted them to go right, because they would go straight from Haley right into Erin. Have mercy on them, Lord, because we weren't.

Layne Doctson was the first seventh grader I ever coached who had a jump shot. It was a beautiful arching shot. Layne could jump out of the gym and led the team in offensive rebounds. She played wing on offense and baseline on defense.

Grace Haynes probably never received close to the credit she deserved. She just quietly went about her job and played her role to perfection. She led the team in rebounding and, as already noted, was a very good shooter. I never remember Grace missing a shot when we really needed the points. She knew her job was to get the rebound and get it to Haley, not to dribble the ball up the court. Although not as tall as her opponent, Grace got the opening tip in all but one game. This also says something about her desire in rebounding. She was our post player on offense and played the middle on defense.

On the second night of tryouts when Meredith Lee was in the sixth grade, Steve came to practice, and I pointed her out and remarked, "That is a warrior." Little did I know. Meredith was an amazingly versatile player. She could post up or step outside and nail a beautiful shot. Prior to the ninth season in summer workouts, she was shooting flat line drives. I told her she could either put a lot of arc on her shots or sit on the bench with me. Her shot became a soft rainbow.

Meredith could rebound and go coast-to-coast with the ball. She was the only post player I coached who could do that and certainly the only one I wanted to do that. Woe be to an opposing player who held the ball within Meredith's reach or one who tried to take it away from her as a poor Wetumpka victim discovered. Mer could also be effective as a ball handler in our stall if one of the guards was out of the game. I regret, for my sake, not hers, that I did not get to coach Meredith's sister, Rachel.

Among David Bethea, Steve, and myself, the starting five was dubbed with the following earned nicknames: Meredith and Grace were "Smash" and "Mash," Haley was "Flash," Erin was "Crash," and Layne was "Cash." They all fit.

A. K. Parrish came into the program with the reputation of being a very good shooter. She was, but she was also an excellent passer and could pivot and protect the ball as well as anyone I ever coached.

Nini Rabsatt-Smith came off the bench in the semis against TPS and revived a sluggish offense as well as garnering ten rebounds.

With these types of players, all of whom were quite bright, made good decisions, and could run the floor, we became a run-and-gun team and were exciting to watch as they worked their ball-handling magic. When we set up in a half-court offense, we did not use set plays, but relied upon the skills and fundamentals learned in summer practice and reinforced during in-season practices. The girls would move the ball around until an opening occurred and then exploit it.

The team called themselves the TJagles over my objections, as I felt it should be all about them. Our motto was "24 Minutes of Torment."

Our tri-captains were Haley, Grace, and Meredith.

As last year's team had gone 13–1 and won the CCC, there was only one way to better it, and the girls did by winning a fourth consecutive CCC and going 14–0 to wrap up a two-year run of 27–1. The team gave up an average of about two and one-half points per quarter.

MA got their running game in gear at STJ and won 36–17. In January, ACA brought an undefeated team to MA and left a defeated one, 22–11. Captain Haley had some stirring words at halftime of the second STJ game, then went out and proceeded to back up her talk with six quick points in the third quarter as MA outscored the Trojans 21–4 in the second half.

In a strange-but-true episode, the girls beat Catholic by the same score both games, 51–8.

In the return match at ACA, we only dressed eight girls due to injuries and illness, but prevailed 36–12. Meredith had 8 points on 57 percent shooting, ten rebounds, two blocks, and three steals. Layne had 15 points and A. K., making her first start of the year, scored 7 points in the first half.

Our last game was a physical battle at Wetumpka, with the MA team prevailing, 27–14. Haley hit five of six for 10 points, adding nine steals, while Erin had five steals.

We went into the tournament with a big bull's-eye on our backs. It was here that Grace showed her reliability as a premier clutch performer, pulling down double-digit rebounds in both games.

In the semis against TPS, MA trailed early and led by only 3 at the end of the third quarter. The team outscored the Wildcats 10–2 in the final quarter, with Layne scoring 6 of the points. Haley had twelve steals, and Nini came off the bench to score 6 points and grab ten rebounds. Trinity was limited to only fourteen shots the entire game.

In a hotly-contested championship game against St. James, Meredith scored 4 of our first 5 points and had a great defensive game with two blocks and four steals.

Trailing by 2, with under two minutes to play, Grace hit a twelve-footer on a great feed from Layne. With under a minute left, Haley made an awesome pass to "Amazing Grace" at near the same spot, and she drained it again to put us ahead to stay. Then came the nail-in-the-coffin on a sidelines out-of-bounds play. In a move that epitomized her career, "Hustling Haley" made the in-bounds pass, then instead of being a spectator as a lot of in-bounders in a similar situation would be, she sprinted to the goal, beating everyone else there to rebound the missed layup and put it back in. Haley had seven steals and ten deflections, and Erin had six steals. St. James could only attempt nineteen shots.

I will never forget two examples of leadership exhibited in this game. At the end of the third quarter, St. James hit a buzzer-beater to tie the game and really fire them and their fans up. On the way to our bench, Haley stopped the team and formed a circle of five and spoke earnestly to them. I have no idea what she said. However, I'll bet dollars to donuts, it started with "Y'all!" They broke the huddle and started to the bench just as the buzzer to start the fourth quarter sounded.

I made my most profound statement to a team when I said to them, "Whatever Haley said, do it!" Think about it; going into the fourth quarter of a championship game, how many coaches would have gone berserk if the team stopped on the way to the bench and did not get to hear "The Master" impart instructions? Folks, I'm not that smart, and I trusted my leader.

Second, St. James wisely did not want to run with us, and they would walk the ball up with each change of possession to them. Each time, Haley, playing the point, would turn around and exhort each of her teammates. How do I describe my appreciation for this type of young lady? I think it quite fitting that Haley scored the first goal in the first game of the season and the last goal in the last game.

Layne was picked on the All-Tournament team, and Haley was selected the tournament's MVP, an award she also won for the season as the team selected her for that honor at our banquet. Tommy and Jenny Andreades were given an award for putting up with me for four years with their two daughters.

Some of the Happiest Years of My Life

And so concluded nine of the happiest years of my life. The teams of players, parents, and coaches compiled a record of 108–18, with nine of those losses coming in a two-year span. Let it be clearly understood: I did not make basketball players. I only tried to help them make themselves.

An interesting breakdown is that the girls were 18–5 against both Catholic and ACA, 20–1 against St. James, and 20–2 versus Trinity.

In those nine years, I coached against approximately 300 girls in CCC play, and to pick the best five was a daunting task. The selections are based only on their play against us, as I rarely saw a player against other teams. It is based upon actual performance, not reputation. I took into consideration things that I value, such as defense, shot selection, which ties in with unselfishness, passing ability, and so on. Some went on to fulfill their potential in high school, and some, for whatever reason, did not.

My first draft choice would be Caroline Wilder, who at this writing is starring at guard at TPS. This is certainly one player that I wished I had had on my team. She saw the floor extremely well and was an excellent passer and never lost her composure. Caroline was a very good shooter but, at the same time, most unselfish. She would hit the floor for a loose ball and could fly down the floor. Those who know her say she has impeccable character and leadership ability, and she is extremely intelligent. I am fortunate I only had to coach against Caroline when she was in the seventh grade. Although her eighth-grade year did not figure in my choosing her as my first draft choice, when she was an eighth grader, she might have played the best game I ever saw a Middle School girl play in the overtime CCC finals against ACA. As I said, I wish she had played for us. Thank goodness, I did not have to coach against her sister, Claire.

Elizabeth Richards of St. James was a smart player who understood how to legally draw fouls and then convert the free throws. Elizabeth was also an excellent shooter, both inside and outside the three-point line, and certainly could not be left unguarded (which we did not!).

Abby Beesley from Catholic was an incredible athlete. Anyone who knows me knows that I would never demean girls basketball, so do not think I am talking down girls when I say that Abby played liked a boy. She was the most physical *good* player we faced. She did it all—shooting, rebounding, and ball handling.

Two girls from ACA complete the "Dream Team" or maybe the "Nightmare Team." Leah Sirmon was another terrific athlete whom, if I remember correctly, started as an eighth grader on ACA's varsity. She was a tall point guard who was a very good floor general. If Leah had a fault, it would be that she was too unselfish and did not shoot enough (thank goodness), as she could literally take a game over. Carlie Ainsworth may have been the best pure shooter I ever coached against, and probably the most consistent three-point shooter I coached against. She was an ideal guard because she could handle the ball so well. She was also a gym rat, which endeared her to me. Carlie was one of only maybe three players that we ever used a zone-and-one defense against, and unlike most players in this situation, she did not lose her composure and heave up chunks, but merely hit the open teammate. Add to that her impeccable character, and you have a winner.

Another young lady must be mentioned whom I would have been honored to coach: Emily Meadows of St. James. Emily lost a leg to cancer as a young child. Did that deter her? Ha! Emily more than held her own and was an amazing competitor.

The two coaches I respected the most were Lisa Vickery of TPS and Patti Turner of ACA. I enjoyed competing against them because both always had their teams well-prepared and fundamentally sound. Watch their teams warm up and you will see sharp passes and correct shooting form. Usually every team would have only one or two girls that did things the correct way, fundamentally, but their teams always had virtually everyone on the team who executed the correct way.

These are the types of teams that worried me, because there was no set pattern and you never knew exactly what was coming.

One coach that I am glad I did not have to coach against is Gennie Honel. Gennie is MSGVB coach and varsity softball coach at TPS. Gennie has done an excellent job with both programs and is an outstanding role model—the type of young lady you would want to coach your daughter.

Other players of note would be Karlin Beck, Sydney Holt, Smith Burley (never saw her make a bad pass), Mary Fran Felder, and Lulu Johnson of Trinity; Taylor Watts, K. Williamson, and Courtney Wilcox of Catholic; Katie Sanderson, Blair and Brandy Brendle, Brooklyn Goodman, and Courtney Barber of ACA; Kelli Christian and Lauren Henry of St. James. Clearly there would be others, but these are the ones who gave us the most trouble.

There is no way I would name an MA All-Star team. In fact, we went out of our way to avoid having a star system. The players were all stars to me, and we focused on being a *team!* There is no way I could name a best defender since they all gave their all. You'd have to say that A.T. was the best shot blocker.

It is equally difficult to pick the best in specific categories, such as best passer or best ball handler. Margaret and Meredith proved to be the most versatile; A.T. and Grace were excellent passers from the post position; Tina Karst, though short in height, had to be the best at setting picks. Haley had to be the biggest (not in size) pest to the opponents' ball handlers. Morgan was unique, as she would switch back-and-forth from point to shooting guard and change her mentality each time. Not many pros can do this. However, since people are interested in offense, I'll say this. Since I am the only person who saw the players every night at practice for nine years and the only one who saw all one hundred twenty-six games, and because I have no family ties and prejudices, I will say that the best pure outside shooters that I coached were Diana and Molly Buss, Ginny Gross, Sydney Anderson, Adele Walter, and Haley Andreades. For anyone I inadvertently left out, please take the tomatoes out of the cans before you throw them, because those cans hurt!

To every girl I was privileged to coach, I want to express my heartfelt appreciation for all that you did for your school. God bless each of you in a very special way.

8

A TYPICAL SEASON OF MSGBB

This philosophy of the game of basketball (and the game of life) and these coaching methods worked for us, and the girls and I were comfortable with them. I'd say that at the end of practice, 99 percent of the time, 99 percent of the girls left laughing and smiling, because we always tried to end practice on a high note. It is my hope that there will be some life lessons for anyone who reads this.

Every "next year's" team started the previous May. I would have a meeting with the girls who wished to try out. The meeting was announced, but I never tried to "recruit" or talk anyone into playing. I just do not believe in doing that. I think it can create problems down the road if you talk someone into playing, then they do not get as much playing time as they expected because of their having been "sold" on the program.

At the meeting, I went over with them my expectations and the conditions and standards to which they would be held. All this information was sent home in writing to the parents, along with a copy for them to sign and send back, indicating they understood the responsibilities for themselves and for their daughters.

We would have four days of practice then tryouts were held on Friday night. Tryouts consisted of skill tests that were based on the drills we had conducted in the practice sessions. Team membership was based *strictly on the results of these tests.* My opinion simply did not enter into team selection. Copies of the results were given to the athletic director, Headmaster, and Middle School director. So far as I know, no parent ever complained about his or her child not making the team. As Wade Segrest said about a child's grade, "The numbers tell the story."

On Saturday night, I would treat the new team to dinner and dessert at Chappies. After we ate, I went over plans for the summer with them. One thing that paid dividends for us was that I asked each girl to get a pair of hand grips and showed them how I wished them to use them each day. Our girls developed incredibly strong wrists, so that once they got a grip on a loose ball or a rebound, it stayed with them.

One night, 250-pound Coach Knute Elmore was walking through the gym, and I asked him to take the ball away from Haley Andreades. Knute slung her around but could never dislodge the ball from her grip. He was amazed. I remember especially three unwise opponents trying that with Mille, Meredith, and Grace resulting in their embarrassment and harm to their bodily health.

We would go to the gym where the girls got their uniforms. The proud parents would be able to photograph them in their uniforms. For many, this was their first experience on a school team. We had one great gag shot in which Lollie and Haley both fit into a uniform jersey. Returning players from the previous year's team got their first choice of numbers. I especially remember one very unselfish moment when Hagan gave up the number she wanted to accommodate a new player.

Each female athlete at MA was expected to put in twelve weight workouts during the summer, while I asked each Middle School girls basketball player to schedule twelve forty-five-minute basketball workouts with me. They could do them individually or in groups. It worked this way: A girl would call me and tell me when she wanted a workout. If gym space was available, that is when we would do it. Abigail Smith practiced at six one morning, as she was leaving on a trip. We had some players working out as late as five in the afternoon. I would not schedule night workouts. Once, Lesley Shinbaum called from Florida to see if she could schedule for the following day, because if not, she was going to stay at the beach an additional day.

The sessions were strictly teaching lessons: fundamentals and drills on how to shoot, dribble, pass, rebound, which foot to have the weight on along the lane on free throws, and so on. We never scrimmaged in the summer. If a girl has some bad basketball habits, playing games and scrimmaging will only reinforce those bad habits. Practice does not make perfect. Practice makes permanent. Perfect practice makes perfect. I remember so well, that E-Bay would not go to something else until she had done a drill the right way. She insisted that I make her do it correctly. All coaches should be so lucky. We certainly did no conditioning in the summer. Why would you? The season was several months away.

We kept free throw charts and shooting charts. Each girl took and recorded a certain number of shots that she would expect to get in a game based on the position she played.

Fridays were known as Friday's Follies. A practice session would last only half the time, and then I'd take the girls next door to the Exxon station and treat them to a snack and soft drink. One day, Syd got and ate a pint, or was it a quart, Sydney, of ice cream! I loved it.

We also did some fun things as a team such as going to the movies or loading up a cheese wagon and going to Peach Park.—YUM, SLURP, BURP!

It is no coincidence that the girls who put the most into the sessions improved the most. Lesley did over ninety workouts one summer, and one hundred seventy-four over two summers. Malone put in over eighty in one summer. (In addition to Lesley, other members of "THE 100 CLUB" were Malone at 156, Haley at 119, Morgan at 116, Meredith, 107, Meghan, 104, and Sydney, 103.) Interestingly, each summer the number of individual workouts increased. The summer before my last season, the girls averaged an incredible forty-two workouts each!

Tribute must be paid to the parents in the summer and during the season. This age group did not drive, so the parents had to bring them and pick them up after practice.

Before fall practice began, each girl would receive a team notebook in a three-ring binder. Our art teacher, Amanda Townsend, would produce a nice drawing that would go on the front of each notebook. The notebook contained no X's or O's. The contents dealt with maxims, quotes, slogans, and team-building and motivational material.

Once volleyball season ended, we began practice. We practiced each night from 5:45 to 7:45. Once we began playing games, we would cut practice on Friday nights by thirty minutes. With this age group, very few training rules had to be employed, but the few rules I did have were strictly enforced. No one was allowed to miss practice unless she was sick (I did not want them there then for their own sake and for that of their teammates) or in cases of family emergencies, such as a death in family. Anyone missing practice for any other reason sat out the next game. Woe be unto anyone missing a game other than being excused. This never happened.

Unfortunately, I had a few isolated unexcused missed practices, and some nice young ladies had to pay the penalty. This hurt them and their parents, and it hurt me just as badly, but I felt that teaching accountability and loyalty to other members of the team was a very important lesson. As anyone can tell you, I played absolutely no favorites in this. I actually looked at it as a reward to those who came to practice to provide them with playing time.

Playing time is not a right, it is a privilege. I do not think it fair to have different requirements for different players, regardless of how good they are and of how it might affect the team's chances of winning. It sends the wrong message. A coach who puts expediency over principle is setting a bad example indeed. This did cost us one game, but it sent a message.

Interestingly, one parent remarked that she did not like the rule, but acknowledged, "At least Coach Jones has rules and he is consistent with them." Players were expected to be on time, and tardiness to practice brought the same consequences, yet somewhat milder in terms of bench time. One year I had a player who was pretty good, but she was invariably late to practice. She would come lackadaisically sauntering in, ten minutes late, no explanation offered, much less an apology. So I responded by her always being the last player on the team to get in a game and then for a limited time. Later, I thought she was getting the message, as she started being on time to practice, so I had her penciled in for more playing time in the next game. Guess what? She was ten minutes later than reporting time for the game. Some you cannot win.

We always started and ended practice in a circle, holding hands. This was to reinforce the concept that it was not my team, but team ownership. At the circle at the end of practice, the captains made any comments they wished; then any player could speak. It was understood that all eyes were on the speaker at all times. Then we had our war cry and went home.

Over 50 percent of our practices were spent on drills and fundamentals. I always gave the first ten minutes for the players to work on what they needed to, and I moved from player to player as needed. It was a treat to watch different players working on ball handling, dribbling, rebounding, shooting, foul shots, and other skills. No player shot out of position. I liked the players to pair up for shooting—one passing, the other shooting. After all, in a game, did you ever see a player materialize on the floor with the ball and shoot? The girls understood that if I had to leave the floor, which I rarely did, they were to practice as if I were there. Occasionally, I would walk out on some pretense and peek in, and never once was there a girl goofing off.

I have sometimes been frustrated when a coach would tell a player what to do without showing them how to do it. The proper way to teach a skill is to tell them, then show them, then have them do it, then correct if necessary, then repeat the process. Then once the player understands the skill, repetition, repetition, repetition. It is not as much fun nor as easy as scrimmaging, but it is much more profitable from a team standpoint and much more fair and considerate of your players in their development. Research has shown that it takes twenty-one days to break an old habit before you can replace it.

We did not have a lot of plays for reasons already stated. Why free up someone if that player had not been taught to shoot properly? We did work a lot on situations that might arise.

We tried to have an element of competition in the drills, with appropriate "rewards" and "consequences." We had some great instances of support in which if one player was left attempting to complete something, the entire team would join in until she would finish.

Many great coaches would disagree with this, but we did not run sprints (running for running's sake) for conditioning. We always had a ball in our hands while running. That way we were practicing our basketball skills while running, making it a realistic basketball situation. One example would be a continuous 3-on-2, 2-on-1 full-court drill. Thus at the same time the girls were running, they were practicing, recognizing, and reacting to gamelike situations. Another favorite drill was "Baldwin County." This was a conditioning drill that encompassed virtually every basketball skill. I can tell you our teams never ran out of gas with this type of conditioning.

We tried to cover every situation that could arise prior to the first game, such as reporting to the scorer's table and the replacement carrying a towel to the girls being replaced.

The team chose their permanent captains prior to the first game. Additionally, I selected game captains for each game. Each year, we would have a "captains" T-shirt. The permanent captains would sign their name and number on the front and the game captains on the back. All except Mary Hendon. She put her name and phone number. That was the first time in about a hundred years that a beautiful young lady had given me her phone number! Recently, I had all my captains shirts made into a beautiful bedspread sewn by Nancy LaPorte of Prattville. Thus, I preserved every signature of every girl I ever coached.

Prior to the first game, we would have a players-parents-coaches dinner. Mothers of the team captains were responsible for organizing the meal. Then while I talked to the parents about the upcoming season, reviewed policies, and covered other matters, the players would go to the gym to warm up. We would then go to the gym and the players whom I had divided up into two teams would compete in a variety of basketball skills. The evening would be concluded with the presentation of awards based on the summer workouts.

Prior to class on the first school day following a game, each girl would get a complete set of individual and team statistics and also a game report card. This report card graded with letter grades (A, B, C, F) along with appropriate comments on the "Seven Secrets of Success." The secrets were defense, rebounding, steals, deflections, floor burns, taking good shots, and not missing layups. It was significant that almost without fail, the girls would look at the team report card before they looked at their individual stats. When that happens, you have a team-first attitude.

The first practice following each game, we would give out awards where appropriate, such as a stuffed frog or kangaroo for any girl who got ten or more rebounds, a stuffed monkey for eight or more steals, a big Band-Aid for x number of floor burns.

At some point in the season, we would take a trip to T-Town, to Dreamland, er, I mean to see a BAMA women's basketball game and incidentally drop by Dreamland to eat.

Periodically, a team newsletter would be mailed to the team parents. It would update them on team and individual stats, team news, upcoming events, and other news.

On Friday night, the night before the CCC tournament, we would hold our last practice, and it was a special one. We would just shoot around for a few minutes, and then I would give them reminders for the next day. After that, we would move to our next segment. We would all sit around in a circle, and first Steve and I would talk to them about how much we appreciated and cared for them. Then he and I would leave the gym, and the girls would remain in a circle and express their support and love for each other. In fact, our team motto for the last season was nothing about basketball or winning, it was, "We love each other."

Last, we took a piece of poster board, and the girls decided and wrote on it our goals for the tournament. They would write things like how few points we were going to give up, rebound margin, turnovers caused, and deflections. We carried the poster with us to the tournament and referred to it after the first game and then at the conclusion.

Game Day

On game day, players could come as early as they liked to loosen up and shoot around. About thirty minutes prior to tip-off, we would go to a meeting place, the training room at MA, and go over reminders. Captains were given time to speak, and any other girl who wished to could also speak. We would form a circle, hold hands, and one of the girls would pray. Then we went out for structured warm-up drills using two WNBA balls for a flashy drill, then competitive drills. The first drill was to attract the other team's attention and to put doubt in their minds. The other was to get the competitive juices flowing before the game started.

I knew what we could do, so I usually watched the other team warm up. I looked for signs that they were organized or whether they had been taught to do the skills the right way.

Except for three games in my tenure, every girl on our teams got in every game. Those three were two championship games and the other decided the regular season championship. So, that means in five championship games, and all but one regular season game, every girl played. Particularly in Middle School, it bothers me when girls do not get in a game. My feeling is that while some may not be as talented as others, they were, after all, picked for the team, and they worked just as hard in practice. I cannot remember subbing ever costing us a game, and it works wonders for team morale. Each girl gets to feel she was part of a victory.

I actually scripted when each girl would go in and for whom and what position she would play. I gave Steve the sub chart, and he took care of getting them in the game. Some years, I would play five subs as a unit and give each a special name, such as The Scream Team and The Swarm Team. They took great pride in completely shutting down an opponent and not allowing a field goal while they were in the game. I actually had other girls asking to be put on that group.

We got every girl in the game during the first half. That way, if she had to enter the game at a crucial point during the second half, she had already been on the floor and gotten rid of the butterflies. It seems inexcusable and unfair to a player to sub her in at a crucial time if she has not already played in the game.

Steve came up with a great idea for substitution protocol. The sub would carry in a towel and hand it to the girl she was subbing for. This was not only a show of practical unity, but in cases of multiple substitution, it guaranteed that we would have five and not more than five on the floor. When a player came off the floor, everyone on the bench at the time stood and gave her a high five.

Unless a sub was already at the scorer's table to come in, a girl who made a turnover would not be jerked out of the game right then. We would wait at least until another dead ball to make a change. I did not want the girls to be afraid to make a mistake. It will negatively affect their play and take the fun out of it for them.

On defense, we were a 1–3–1 zone team. In only three games did we vary from that—when Sarah took Elizabeth Richards and, frankly, they had no one else who was a concern from us. The other two were when Anna took Kelli Christian of STJ and Mille took Carlie Ainsworth, and we could do this because in both cases Hagan could cover both post and point. Other teams knew exactly what we would do on defense, but it did them no good because our girls took so much pride in their defense and because they could not really simulate our defense in practice.

We actually considered it an insult when anyone attempted a legitimate shot against us, and in a lot of games, by the second half, they were so tired of us being in their face, they would throw the ball in the general direction of the basket just to get rid of it. We called them "chunks" and kept up with how many they took.

In defensive practice, we would always stop and determine when someone got an open shot, analyze it, and make the adjustment. A lot of teams start out playing tough defense but slack off in the second half. We played with the same intensity throughout. We termed it playing as if we were one point ahead with twelve seconds left the entire game. We were especially cognizant of how many shots were *allowed*, turnovers caused, and deflections in the fourth quarter.

We rarely pressed, because our half-court defense was so good. We wanted the other team to try to attack it. About the only time we would press was when the other team least expected it, as in the final CCC game in which we pressed when we were 4 points ahead with under thirty seconds left. Do what they do not expect, when they do not expect it. Another mantra of ours was that while offense brings the fans in, defense wins championships. Your defense should never have an off game. A lot of teams say it, but we played it—*Defense!*

Gene Stallings famously said many times, "Schemes don't win games, players making plays win games." Our teams bought into that. We had certain formations and sets, but few actual called plays. We had an opening tip play that, if we got the tip, would usually get us a shot either from the corner or a layup. We had one sideline out-of-bounds play and two sideline out-of-bounds formations against pressure. We used four out-of-bounds plays under the opponent's basket and one set against a press. We always had a way to get the ball in and get it right back to the point guard who had thrown it in. With at least two of Lizzie, Lesley, Morgan, Haley, and Erin, a team was committing suicide by pressing us.

In half-court, we would set up according to the defense, and from there the players took over. We would drive to the gap and dish off; we would "drag," that is, dribble away from a spot, and another player would fill the spot for a pass back. A wing would drive the baseline and pass to the opposite post or opposite corner. (Sarah Reid was so good at this, it looked like the maneuver was invented with her in mind.) Or the wing would drive and pass to the strong side high post, as Layne and Grace worked it in the final CCC game.

In a double high post, a post player with the ball would pass from her elbow to the opposite wing or corner, or go backdoor to the strong side wing cutting to the basket. Folks, that's it, and I never had to call anything!

Against a man, we used simple picks and rolls and scissors-cut off a high post. I very rarely would call out anything, as players had seen everything in practice and knew how to react, and with the endless repetition of drills on the right way to perform the various skills, the girls automatically responded to situations and took what was there. Also, we would rarely call out individual instructions to a girl who was playing.

We did have a delay game with any ball handler having the option to break for the basket when the opening was there.

We would run a play at the end of a quarter that was essentially nothing more than a variation of the drag-throw back. We would hold the ball until there were twelve seconds left and then initiate the play. This would give us time to rebound and put back up a missed shot, but not give the opponents time to score regardless. Watching videos of the games, I could not help but smile, as in several games, when we were running the clock down, a couple of the same voices were heard yelling, "Shoot!" What was that thing Coach Stallings said about listening to the spectators?

While on the subject, the girls really do not hear any instructions from the stands. I have asked them, and they would reply, "What are you talking about? I didn't hear anything." The only exception to that was one game in which there were very few people in the stands, and a mother was constantly yelling at her daughter. The girl finally stopped in the middle of the court and screamed, "Mother, shut up!" While I do not approve of speaking to a parent that way, this time it might have been justified. This is something that really bothers me—a parent in the stands loudly fussing at their child. It almost seems their own self-worth is defined by how their offspring is performing.

At a VGBB game a few years ago, I was sitting in the stands by two of our lady fans who did not know a basketball from a cantaloupe, yet they were constantly yelling at the officials about an opposing player's "three seconds in the lane." It was embarrassing, because the girl was not in the lane. She was posted just above the foul line. I moved my seat.

Our girls were made to understand at the beginning of each season that they could only do one thing well, so they had to decide if they were going to play, coach, or referee. We had a standing rule that any player who indicated displeasure with an official's call, no matter how atrocious she thought it was, was not allowed to show any negative emotion. It is simply poor sportsmanship. This was one mistake that would get the young lady instant time on the pine. I have watched two MA guys and one MA girl, well, now, two, who would have been very rested at the conclusion of games unless they repented. I call it the "Oscar Robertson Syndrome." Oscar Robertson was one of the greatest of all basketball players, but he "never committed a foul." Just ask him. It was always the official's mistake. If one official had just had the guts that my niece had when she was calling intramural guys games at The University of Alabama, it might have cured him.

A few years ago, David Bethea and I were going to an MA girls game. We had had a very good year, losing rarely, but we really did not lose any games. The officials took them, according to a few MA parents. I told David on the way to the game that if we should happen to lose, I hope that it would be accepted that we just got beat. We did lose, and guess what? It was the officials' fault. Hey, that is true everywhere, and it is sad. I just want MA to be a cut above all the other schools.

I always have felt that a coach constantly yelling at and questioning officials has negative results. Those people are human, and if it comes down to a crucial call in the final seconds, who do you think is going to get the call: the coach who has complained the entire game or the other coach? Also, if a coach gets upset, the players get upset, and it affects his or her play. I've seen a lot of coaches who spend more time officiating than they do coaching. Watch Anthony McCall. Rarely does he yell at an official, but during a free throw or a dead ball, he will talk quietly to the nearest official. It is more effective. They really do not like to be shown up.

Certainly, there are showboat officials and those with an attitude, but it does no good to incur their enmity. At the same time, there are showboat coaches who want to make sure that the fans are aware of their presence. They throw out the words *I* and *me* a lot.

Joe Torre, or "Mr. Torre," as Derek Jeter always called him, once went on the field during a game and approached the umpire. Joe told him, "There are 50,000 fans in the stands. They did not come to see me manage nor you to umpire."

So what kind of coach was I? I think I was a teaching coach, a good practice coach. I think I was an adequate game coach. I never believed I could outsmart another coach in a game, but I did feel I could outwork them during the off season, and it really was not work for me but pure enjoyment. I believe we were successful in terms of wins and losses because we had good players who sacrificed their time in the summer to get better and who practiced so well that they automatically reacted in games.

Pat Summit, along the lines of other great coaches, remarked, "Teams are made in the winter, but players are made in the summer." I see myself, along with being a teacher, as an encourager. I was not a chewing-out type of coach, I rarely fussed. When a girl did something the right way, I made sure that she knew that I saw it and appreciated it. I think there are coaches who over-coach in a game.

I joked with the girls and in practice; we played a lot of fun games like "basketball football" in which the players did not realize they were practicing and learning basketball skills while competing and having fun. I did some written surveys with them to help them know their teammates better. I like to think the girls won the games in spite of me and just hoped they did not realize it at the time.

There are two more thoroughly enjoyable incidents that I wish to mention. At the end of the third season, we had a mother-team game. Brittany's mom, Melody, could still play. She could have played on our team. Lani's mom, also named Melody, was a terrific defensive player. If one of the girls came into her area, she just grabbed them and held on. The other occasion involved the Andreades sisters. When Haley was in the seventh grade, we scrimmaged the JV team of which Laura was a member. You talk about two girls getting after each other! There was no quarter asked and none given.

Some of my favorite memories are of our team Christmas parties. The day we got out for the holidays, we would go to Jason's to eat, have a good time, and exchange gifts. Those were fun times.

So why give it up? You have to understand that I am a dying breed among coaches, a dinosaur. I am old, old school. Just like I believed in wearing a coat and tie to all games, my philosophy on discipline and what is acceptable is also ancient. Basically, I gave it up because of off-the-court issues, one in particular, that I just got tired of dealing with. I still loved practices and games and cherished the relationship that a coach has with his players. I miss that, but the thorns were starting to catch up with the roses. No doubt, these were the happiest nine years of my happy thirty-five years at MA.

I am concerned about the future of girls basketball at MA. Not the coaches; we have excellent girls basketball coaches. The decreasing numbers of players are disturbing. In asking girls and the parents of girls who gave up basketball, I got two constant answers. Girls do not like to run. Now, we have a highly successful girls track program, but it is different than basketball in that no one sits on a bench. Everyone participates in every meet. The second is that girls do not like to get hit and have other players' hands on them. Unfortunately, girls basketball is becoming more of a physical game than a finesse one. I think part of the blame is that most officials are guys who themselves played rough-and-tumble basketball when they were younger.

A few have said that on the varsity level, the time constraints are not worth it, especially during Christmas vacation when there is little if any time for family trips. I really think the CCC Christmas tournament should be abolished. The in-town teams play each other enough as it is without adding another game with each other. One problem at MA is that there is not a girls basketball coach on campus. There is no one there during the school day to promote and push the program. There is no one to see the girls on campus and to be able to talk with them between classes about things in their lives. It is not an insurmountable barrier, but coupled with these other reasons, it is a problem.

I'll repeat that coaching at MA was a wonderful experience for me, and my heartfelt appreciation goes out to the girls and their parents who made it so enjoyable. Another thanks to Steve and Julibeth, to John Tatum and to all the coaches on staff for their support, and to the teachers who kept me informed about the girls. A final thanks to the cheerleaders and their coaches, who got up early on some cold Saturday mornings and faithfully attended our games, cheering us on.

9

DRIPS FROM JONES'S JUG

My Favorite Quotations

- Never squat with your spurs on.
- Everyone doesn't share your passions and interests. Remember that in your conversations.
- There is nothing more unwelcome than unasked-for advice or opinions.
- Always drink upstream from the herd.
- You never hear, "It's only a game" from the person who is winning.
- How many times do you say the word *I* every day, as in "I did," "I was," "I," "I," "I." Gets kind of tiresome to listen to. Also, the middle letter in the word "sin" is "i."
- If you are talking, you are not learning.
- Seat belts are not as confining as wheelchairs.
- The trouble with bucket seats is that not everyone has the same-sized bucket.
- Never talk about your children, team, etc., unless you are first asked. Then keep it mercifully brief.
- You can tell more about a person by what he says about others than by what others say about him.
- The promises you make do not say much about you. The promises you keep say everything about you.

- In just a few minutes you can ruin a reputation for life that it has taken all your life to build.
- It's not what you have in your life, but who you have in your life that counts.
- In forty years, we will have millions of old ladies running around with wrinkled tattoos.
- Just think, if it were not for marriage, men would go through life thinking they had no faults at all.
- Did you ever notice that the Roman numeral for forty is XL?
- Speak well of your enemies. After all, you made them.
- Blessed are those who, when they have absolutely nothing worthwhile to say, abstain from giving wordy evidence of the fact.
- Tact is for people not witty enough to be sarcastic.
- An excuse is the skin of a reason stuffed with a lie.
- A lot of people enjoy the comfort of an opinion without the discomfort of thought.
- Read health books and die of a misprint.
- If we are to love our neighbors as ourselves, we must accept people as they are and not demand that they conform to our own image.
- Never pet a dog that is foaming at the mouth.
- Rule number one: The boss is always right. Rule number two: If the boss is ever wrong, refer back to rule number one.
- Be careful about blowing your own horn. It is much better if someone else does it for you.
- A good sermon has a good beginning, a good ending, and the two are as close together as possible.
- Tell the truth and your troubles are behind you. Lie and they are ahead of you.
- We are known by how we treat people.
- What we say about others says more about us than it does them.
- Whatever you want to do, do it now. There are only so many tomorrows.

- Be good to your children. They will choose your nursing home.
- Arguing with an idiot means two idiots are arguing.
- When you get old and people ask you how you feel, may God give you the grace not to tell them.
- Bear the burden of discipline, or you will bear the burden of regret.
- When a colleague comes in to speak to you, be polite and turn away from that screen. That computer will always be there. Your friend won't.
- Some people obviously got their college major in "How to Be Offended."
- God put our eyes in front of our head so we can see where we are going, not where we have been.
- Trust God, but lock your car.
- Some people are like the rooster who thinks the sun comes up every morning just to hear himself crow.
- If you could buy them for what they are worth and sell them for what they think they are worth, you would be a jillionaire.
- Never trust a man whose belt buckle is bigger than his head.
- You cannot always control your circumstances, but you can control your attitude toward them.
- Adversity reveals true character.
- It's not what you get out of something that matters, it's what you put into it.
- If at first you don't succeed, skydiving is not for you.
- There are two excellent ways for arguing with women. Neither one of them work.
- If you tell the truth, you don't have to remember what you said.
- Never take a sleeping pill and a laxative on the same night.
- No one ever solves anything by worrying about the past.
- Some people spend their life standing at the complaint counter.
- Just be yourself. Everyone else is taken.

- We would not spend nearly as much time worrying about what people think of us if we know how little they actually did.
- A school is a building that has tomorrow in it.
- A person is often deemed wise by what he or she doesn't say.
- People spend money they don't have to buy things they don't want to impress people they don't like.
- Look people in the eye during conversations.
- Be a good listener.
- Write thank you notes and mean it.
- For true insights, observe people on the golf course.
- Live a healthy life, die anyway.
- Don't talk too much. You will eventually run out of people who will listen to you.
- Remember, whenever you point your finger in accusation at someone else, you have three fingers pointing back at yourself.
- What you do not say, you do not have to wish you could take back. A bell cannot be unrung.
- If Harry Potter is so dad gummed magical, why doesn't he fix his own eyesight?
- What is it about a cell phone that makes guys pace when they talk? Ever see a guy not walk when he is on one?
- There are no pockets in shrouds.
- Some days you're the windshield; other days you are the bug.
- Be careful what you wish for. You may get it, but then you may not want what you get.
- We can control our choices, but we cannot control the consequences of our choices.
- To be happy, have something to do, have something to look forward to, and have someone to love.
- To be successful, do what you are supposed to do, when you are supposed to do it, the way you are supposed to do it, and do it that way all the time.
- A camel is a horse designed by a committee.

- A committee is a group of the unwilling appointed by the incompetent to do the unnecessary.
- If you do not go to other people's funerals, then they will not come to yours.
- The newest conservative is a liberal who just got mugged.
- It is easier to leave angry words unspoken than to mend a heart these words have broken.
- The only way to get things finished, is to get things started
- Grudges are like babies. The more you nurse them, the bigger they get.
- If you want to be successful. get out of facebook and in to someone's face.

My Favorite Bumper Stickers

- POLITICALLY INCORRECT, AND PROUD OF IT
- HANG UP AND DRIVE

My Favorite Insult

- May the fleas of a thousand camels infest your armpits.

My Final Salute

- "Happy trails, and may the good Lord take a liking to you." Roy Rogers
- "Have a great life, and you will if you are just half as happy as my thirty-five years have been at MA." TJ

10

BEYOND RETIREMENT

I really missed a golden opportunity the summer following my retirement. My daughter-in-law, Julibeth, had come down to help me with the many complexities involved in changing insurance. We were coming down the stairs from the business office at school and an MA teacher and a former teacher were in conversation at the foot of the stairs. I made the introductions, and we moved on.

I wish I had just introduced Julibeth as "Mrs. Jones." Boy, would that have caused a stir. "Old Man Jones has himself a young wife." That would have been classic!

When you are criticized, first consider the source. Then consider what their agenda is. Third, never bother with criticism from the uniformed who think they are informed. Fourth, Remember those who know the least, know it the loudest.

To all of you between the ages of nine and ninety, please allow me to quote my childhood cowboy hero Roy Rogers in saying, "Happy trails, and may the good Lord take a liking to you."

I want to add a special message to my former students: I am going to pahk the cah in Hahvahd Yahd and have ah bahtle of pop, so, CA MAHN, CHUMS!

INDEX

Virden, Margaret, 82, 83, 84, 90
Virden, Mille, 75, 92, 99
volleyball teams, 63
Vucovich, Meagan, 69–70, 71

W
Walker, Malone, 77, 81
Walker, Sara, 45
Walter, Adele, 51–52, 81, 82, 90
warm-up drills
    basketball, 97–98
    game day activities, 97–101
Watts, Taylor, 90
weight workouts during summer, 92
Weil, Dustin, 44
Wetumpka, school basketball team,
    83, 85, 86
Whale Tail, 37
Who Moved My Cheese? (Johnson
    (Spencer) and Blanchard), 10
Wilcox, Courtney, 90
Wilder, Caroline, 88
Wilder, Clair, 88
Williamson, K., 90
Wills, Whitney, 25
Wilson, Lillian, 42
Wilson, Wesley, 42
Wimbererly, Beth Weiss, 47
Wise, Blaine, 76
Wolf, Cameron, 70
Womack, Damion, 25
women, policy of hiring, 13
Woods, Rolanda, 31
"Worship the Sun God" team, 61

Y
yellow slips, 1
Young, Florence Ellen, 44